Renewing Earth's Waters

ENVIRONMENT AT RISK

Renewing
Earth's
Waters

CHRISTINE PETERSEN

Marshall Cavendish
Benchmark
New York

Other Marshall Cavendish Offices:
Marshall Cavendish International (Asia) Private Limited, 1 New Industrial Road, Singapore 536196 • Marshall Cavendish International (Thailand) Co Ltd. 253 Asoke, 12th Flr, Sukhumvit 21 Road, Klongtoey Nua, Wattana, Bangkok 10110, Thailand • Marshall Cavendish (Malaysia) Sdn Bhd, Times Subang, Lot 46, Subang Hi-Tech Industrial Park, Batu Tiga, 40000 Shah Alam, Selangor Darul Ehsan, Malaysia

Marshall Cavendish is a trademark of Times Publishing Limited

All websites were available and accurate when this book was sent to press.

Library of Congress Cataloging-in-Publication Data
Petersen, Christine.
Renewing Earth's waters / by Christine Petersen.
p. cm.— (Environment at risk)
Includes bibliographical references and index.
Summary: "Provides comprehensive information on the interrelationship of the natural world, environmental problems both natural and man-made, the relative risks associated with these problems, and solutions for resolving and/or preventing them"—Provided by publisher.
ISBN 978-0-7614-4004-8
1. Water conservation. 2. Water quality. 3. Watershed management. 4. Environmental protection. I. Title.
TD388.P48 2010
333.91'16—dc22
2008020905

Editor: Christine Florie
Publisher: Michelle Bisson
Art Director: Anahid Hamparian
Series Designer: Sonia Chaghatzbanian

Expert Reader: Dr. Hugo A. Loaiciga, Professor, Department of Geography, University of California at Santa Barbara

Photo research by Marybeth Kavanagh
Cover photo by age fotostock/SuperStock
The photographs in this book are used by permission and through the courtesy of:
SuperStock: Gary Brettnacher, 2; Fogstock LLC, 24; Dembinsky Photo Assoc.: 71; NASA/Phil Degginger, 6; Gary Meszaros, 32; Photo Researchers, Inc.: Lynette Cook, 9; Gary Hincks, 11, 15; Robert Brook, 37; David R. Frazier Photolibrary, Inc., 57; Calvin Larsen, 77; Inga Spence, 79; USGS: John Evans, 13; Corbis: Lowell Georgia, 17; Mark Hanauer, 73; Roberstock.com: Jerry Monkman, 22; Animals Animals-Earth Scenes: Michael Gadomski, 26; C.C. Lockwood, 45; Peter Arnold Inc.: WILDLIFE, 28; Alamy: Rick & Nora Bowers, 30; Minden Pictures: Flip Nicklin, 34; The Image Works: David M. Jennings, 41; Ilja C. Hendel/VISUM, 50; AP Photo: Key West Citizen, Rob O'Neal, 46; PhotoEdit: Dennis MacDonald, 61; NASA: Goddard Space Flight Center Scientific Visualization Studio, 63; Mira.com: Tyler Campbell, 64; Designed by Conservation Design Forum, Elmhurst, IL. www.cdfinc.com, 83

Printed in Malaysia (T)
135642

Contents

One

The Water Planet

On December 21, 1968, the National Aeronautic and Space Administration (NASA) rocket ship *Apollo 8* was launched into flight toward the Moon. As the first manned spacecraft to orbit the Moon, an important aspect of the historic flight's mission was to search for lunar landing sites that astronauts could use on future flights. Along the way, the three American astronauts took dozens of photographs of Earth.

Two days after the astronauts returned home, NASA allowed newspapers to print a photo that quickly became famous. It shows the gray landscape of the Moon directly below *Apollo 8*. In the distance, Earth is a half circle of brilliant color, partly shadowed by the Moon. Swirls of clouds eddy like white rivers over blue oceans. It is breathtaking against the darkness of space.

Upon viewing this image, people around the world gained their first real grasp of the delicate beauty of our planet. Four years later, in 1972, *Apollo 17* was able to collect even more stunning high-resolution photos. This time the entire planet was

This image of Earth, released in 2001, is similar to that of *Apollo 8's* in 1968. It is clear that Earth is a planet of water.

visible, brightly lit by sunlight. These iconic images of Earth have become familiar to children and adults in many parts of the world. What do they reveal about our planet? Each person may take away some unique impression, but one fact is hard to ignore: Earth is a water planet.

Three States of Water

Earth's solar system has planets, moons, comets, and asteroids that contain water vapor or are covered in ice. Recent findings even suggest that Mars once had liquid water. Yet Earth may be unique because water has been present in all three states—solid, liquid, and gas—throughout much of its 4.6 billion-year history. The total volume of water on Earth's surface is 332.5 million cubic miles (1.39 billion cubic kilometers). (A cubic unit is the equivalent of a box that is one unit long, one wide, and one high.) This amount is so great that if Earth's surface were flat, water would blanket the planet to a depth of more than 1.7 miles (2.7 km).

Most of the water on Earth is in the liquid state. Some water is frozen as ice sheets and glaciers, most of which are found at the poles—on the continent of Antarctica to the south, and on the island of Greenland and the Arctic Ocean in the north. Although the ratio of liquid to frozen water has varied throughout Earth's long history, depending on global climate, liquid water currently covers approximately 74 percent of the planet. Additionally, water is always present in the atmosphere as a gas. This represents a small percentage of Earth's total water supply, but it is the source of rain and other precipitation such as snow and hail. Global wind currents move this water around the planet.

Amazingly, yet more liquid water is held far beneath the surface, in Earth's mantle. This layer lies between the crust (a thick layer of rocks found under the continents and oceans) and the molten core of the planet. Scientists recently found evidence of a huge supply of water in the mantle under eastern Asia, equivalent in volume to 20 percent of the water in Earth's oceans. Much more water than this may be present but is yet undiscovered.

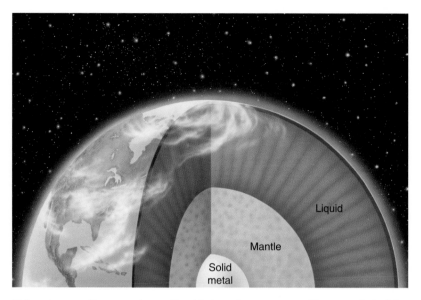

This cutaway diagram shows Earth's interior structure. The mantle holds a vast amount of liquid water.

Salt Water Versus Fresh

Water, water everywhere,
Nor any drop to drink.

English poet Samuel Taylor Coleridge wrote these two lines in the late 1790s as part of his long poem *The Rime of the Ancient Mariner.* It told the tale of a ship full of sailors (mariners) who found themselves stranded in the middle of the ocean. For days, no wind blew to fill their sails. As their tongues "withered at the root" and their "black lips baked," the mariners lamented the irony of being surrounded by water—yet having none that they could drink to survive.

More than two hundred years later, Coleridge's lines are still quoted to describe situations in which a person is surrounded by a lot of something that they cannot have. Believe it or not, it is an appropriate description of the situation humanity faces with water. A huge proportion of Earth's water—96.5 percent—is in the oceans. Seawater has a high

We Are Water

Water not only surrounds us; it is part of every living thing. On average, 60 percent of human body weight is from water. Our bodies constantly use water to regulate temperature and to remove wastes, so it must be replaced regularly. To survive, each person needs about a gallon (3.8 liters) per day for drinking; 13 gallons (49 L) is more realistic in providing for basic hygiene, bathing, and food preparation. Plants also store water in their tissues, and we obtain some of our water by eating them. Approximately 85 percent of the weight of an apple is water; the stem of a saguaro cactus may be as much as 90 percent water.

salinity, meaning that it contains large concentrations of dissolved salts. Average salinity in the oceans is 35,000 parts per million (ppm). (Salinity of the Great Salt Lake, in Utah, can be more than 250,000 ppm—in other words, the ratio of salts to water is one to four!) Living things need salts, including sodium chloride (table salt), potassium, and calcium. Salts help to conduct electricity in cells, allowing nerves to transmit impulses and facilitating many other cell functions. When the human body takes in excess salts, however, the kidneys must work harder to expel them—and in the process, will deplete water. To be healthy, humans (and most animals that live on land) must drink fresh water. This is defined as water with less than 1,000 ppm of salts.

Rivers contribute a large measure of the salts that make ocean water so saline. As rivers flow, they slowly erode the landscape. Minerals contained within rocks are released in the process. Water is sometimes called the universal solvent because of its ability to dissolve a wide variety of substances. Salts readily dissolve in water and are carried downstream. Although salt concentrations may be low in a single river, the oceans receive loads of salt from many rivers over long periods of time. Worldwide, approximately 4 billion tons of salts are transported to the oceans each year. Ocean salt concentrations do not increase too rapidly because each year some salts are deposited in newly forming sediments on the sea floor.

A Precious Resource

The ability to get water from a faucet or the store can be deceptive. In truth, freshwater is a precious resource. Less than 3 percent of all water on the planet is fresh. Two-thirds of this is frozen into ice sheets and glaciers. The remaining fresh water, in liquid state, is found in groundwater or surface water. Ninety-nine percent of all liquid freshwater is stored as groundwater, in rocks just below Earth's surface. Wells can be drilled to access some groundwater supplies; others are out of reach, located as much as several miles below the surface. (Mantle water, mentioned previously, is a separate supply of water located below Earth's thick crust. It is not accessible to people.)

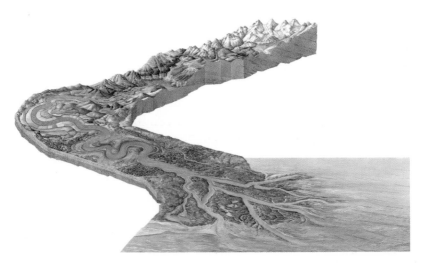

This illustration depicts a river as it moves across the landscape from higher-elevation headwaters (source) to its mouth at the sea.

Counting Parts

Parts per million is a ratio used to compare the concentration of a pollutant to the substance in which it is found (usually water or soil). It can express very dilute concentrations. Imagine that you are testing for Contaminant X in a lake. You get a result of 23 ppm. This result finds that of every million particles in your sample, 23 are Contaminant X. The rest are water or other particles.

Some pollutants, such as mercury, must be measured to even smaller concentrations. Mercury is a naturally occurring metal that is often used in dry-cell batteries and electronics. It is also released when fossil fuels are burned and during other industrial processes. Atmospheric mercury can be carried over long distances. It eventually falls on land, where microbes in soil and water convert it to an organic form (combined with carbon) called methylmercury. Small plankton (floating micro-organisms) eat the microbes, and they are in turn eaten by larger animals in the water. In this way, mercury is passed up the food chain. Methylmercury levels are especially high in the bodies of predatory fish and large birds. Humans absorb methylmercury by eating fish and shellfish. These are healthy foods that people can safely eat in small amounts. Excess exposure to mercury, however, can cause damage to the nervous system and kidneys, especially in developing fetuses. For this reason, the U.S. Environmental Protection Agency (EPA) has set 2 parts per billion (ppb) as the safe limit for mercury in drinking water. Contact your local health department to find out more about safe fish consumption and mercury.

Only 0.008 percent of the planet's total water supply is in sur-face waters—wetlands, rivers, and lakes (including man-made reservoirs).

Water on the Move
Water moves wherever it is found: over and through the soil, in and out of living things, and between land, the atmosphere, groundwater, surface water, and oceans. This continuous move-ment is known as the global water cycle.

The Sun is the main source of energy for Earth. When sunlight heats Earth's surface, it causes water to evapo-rate. Evaporation is the conversion of liquid water to water vapor (a gas). Each year, an average of 105,500 cubic miles (440,000 cubic km) of water is evaporated from the oceans; more evaporation occurs from freshwater, frozen water (such as snowpack or glaciers), soil, and the bodies of plants. (Plant evaporation is called transpiration.)

Water vapor rises into the atmosphere. At higher altitudes it cools and condenses into liquid form. Condensed water

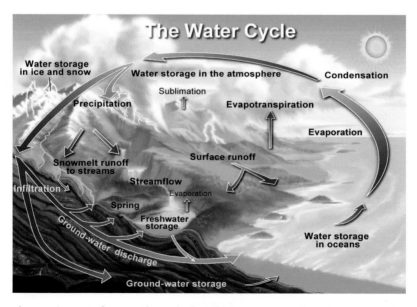

The movement of water through the environment is called the water cycle.

particles are present in the atmosphere even on a clear day, but water molecules also have a tendency to combine with particles in the air. Millions of particles make up each water droplet, and these cling together to form clouds. Winds can carry clouds over long distances. Eventually, condensed water falls from clouds as precipitation. Temperature determines whether this will become rain, snow, sleet, or hail. A large share of all precipitation falls directly onto the ocean. When precipitation falls on land, it may seep down into the soil (infiltrate), run off over the surface of the land, or evaporate back to the atmosphere.

Infiltration is the movement of water from the ground surface into the underlying soil. This is important to plants: a single birch tree may collect 80 gallons (300 L) of water on a warm summer day. Up to a point, the molecular attraction between water and soil particles, along with capillary forces, keeps water from moving farther. When the soil water layer becomes full, however, the forces of gravity and air pressure from above begin to push water deeper into the ground. Percolation is the name for this movement of water through soils and rock after it has infiltrated the surface.

Soil layers usually extend no more than 6.6 feet (2 meters) below the surface. Beneath that are layers of rock. Percolation occurs mostly into porous rocks, such as sandstone, which contain small spaces between the grains. These spaces might be microscopic—but so are water molecules. They can travel through and saturate (fill) the rock. Some types of limestone rock are permeable (allow water through them) because they slowly dissolve when exposed to acidic water. Harder rocks with cracks may have spaces that hold some water as well.

Eventually, percolating water always strikes a layer of rock through which it cannot move. Water fills the porous rocks above this impermeable layer (just as a bathtub fills from the bottom up). The top of the saturated layer in a particular region is called the water table. Water tables rise and fall over time and in different areas of Earth. If there is a great deal of precipitation in a region, or the impermeable layer is not deep underground, the water table may rise all the way to the surface.

The movement of slightly acidic water over limestone causes the rock to slowly erode. Small joints and fissures form, as well as magnificent caves.

Groundwater is removed in two ways: it flows out by the force of gravity, or is pulled out when people operate wells. Within the saturated layer, groundwater flows laterally along the impermeable layer, following the slope of the land. It might take thousands of years for water to travel a few hundred yards in denser rocks, while very porous rocks allow water to move comparatively quickly, on the order of a few yards a day. Erosion and other forces, such as earthquakes, often expose the saturated layer. This allows water to seep onto the surface. Such locations are called springs. Springs provide water to rivers and lakes and can be especially important during droughts. The reverse is also true—beds of rivers and lakes often recharge (refill) groundwater.

Climate has a strong impact on an area's water table, with drought or periods of high rainfall causing noticeable changes. Over time, however, the rate of groundwater recharge roughly equals the rate that is flowing out through springs. Humans can significantly alter this equilibrium by overusing groundwater.

A groundwater supply large enough to meet human needs is called an aquifer. In 2000 aquifers provided 21 percent of the water used in the United States. Aquifers vary in size. Some are no larger than a city block and can only provide enough water for a few families. Others, like the Ogallala Aquifer, are massive and contain water that has been accumulating for millennia. The Ogallala has an area of approximately 174,000 square miles (450,000 square km) and lies under parts of eight states—from Wyoming and South Dakota south to Texas. Heavy use of water from the Ogallala, especially for irrigation of crops in that dry region, has caused the aquifer's water table to fall by approximately 150 feet (46 m) in the past century.

Runoff is a part of the water cycle that takes place when the soil is saturated. Runoff occurs as sheet flow, which is a thin layer of water that spreads across the landscape, pulled downslope by the force of gravity. It usually flows toward channels in the landscape, which then become streams. Water gathers in the lowest points of any landscape as wetlands, ponds, or lakes. Eventually, a large portion of runoff makes its way to the ocean.

A Dose of Reality

In the early 1970s, those stunning images of Earth from space were contrasted by data exposing the globally poor conditions of groundwater, wetlands, rivers, lakes, and oceans. World population was one of the major causes of water pollution. In 1900, 1.6 billion people lived on the planet. In 1970 that number had more than doubled, to 3.9 billion, and was continuing to increase at an extremely rapid rate. Instead of living mostly in rural areas, 69 percent of the U.S. population had clustered into metropolitan areas—cities and suburbs. Forty percent of those North American cities had populations greater than one million.

Lifestyles had changed, as well, due in large part to the Industrial Revolution that began early in the nineteenth century. Work that was once entirely done by hand—crushing grain, spinning yarns, smelting metals, packing meat, and much more—was now done in mills and factories. Advancements in farm machinery increased food production. By the mid–twentieth century,

Tailings from the Tilden Copper Mine and Mill in Ishpeming, Michigan, have polluted a nearby body of water.

cars and airplanes had become common forms of transportation. Electricity was available in most homes in developed countries. The field of chemistry was booming as well. Among the innovations were pesticides that made crops almost insect-free. Pharmaceuticals used in treatments for an increasingly wider range of human diseases were also developed.

Pollution was the price for this great expansion in population and industry. Although natural processes such as erosion can affect water quality, pollution refers to damage done by humans. It makes water unhealthy for people to use and affects the condition of natural aquatic environments. In the 1960s and 1970s, the United States faced crisis conditions in many of its freshwater and seaside communities.

A striking example is the Potomac River, which begins just north of Washington, D.C., and flows into the Chesapeake Bay. Despite its prominent location near the nation's capital, in the early 1970s the Potomac was severely polluted. For

17

decades, sewage and sediments had washed into the river. Sewage includes household wastes from toilets and drains, industrial wastes, and anything that washes off paved surfaces and rooftops during rainfall—trash, oil, pet excreta, organic deposits such as fallen leaves, and more. Sediments are particles such as sand, silt, and dust. These are washed or blown by wind off farm fields and paved surfaces. Fish populations in the Potomac began to die due to the sewage and sediment pollution. The water was declared unsafe for swimming, and additional treatment was required to make it safe for drinking.

Ohio's Cuyahoga River, which empties into Lake Erie, caught national attention in a more unusual way. Sections of the river were so thickly covered with oil and chemicals that they caught fire several times. Around that same time, high levels of mercury were measured in large oceangoing fish. Drinking-water samples throughout the nation showed evidence of hazardous chemicals that threatened human health and the environment. It was time for a change.

Taking Action

For most of U.S. history, the individual states had been responsible for maintaining the quality of water within their boundaries. In 1948 the first legislation was passed allowing the federal government to act on sources of pollution that affected human health. This law, the Federal Water Pollution Control Act of 1948 (FWPCA), is the basis for all current water legislation in the United States. The FWPCA also provided some funding for sewage treatment plants, because sewage had already been identified as a primary source of water pollution.

President Lyndon B. Johnson approved amendments to the FWPCA in 1965. Called the Water Quality Act of 1965, these amendments established the first water quality standards—measurements of water quality, and goals for improvement—that could be enforced by the federal government. The introduction of federal standards set a firm expectation that the states would collaborate in preventing pollution, while also working to protect public health.

Polls conducted in 1971 showed that 68 to 78 percent of Americans were concerned about cleaning up water and air pollution—even if it meant passing new laws and paying additional taxes. The Clean Water Act of 1972 provided firm criteria that scientists and policy makers believed could be used to finally reduce water pollution. Yet despite public approval, the legislation almost did not pass. Faced with heavy financial burdens from the Vietnam War, President Richard M. Nixon vetoed the bill because of its costs. Congress overrode his decision. Senator Edmund Muskie of Maine spoke passionately on the subject, saying:

> Can we afford clean water? Can we afford rivers and lakes and streams and oceans which continue to make possible life on this planet? Can we afford life itself? Those questions were never asked as we destroyed the waters of our Nation, and they deserve no answers as we finally move to restore and renew them.

Many factors influence water quality, determining whether it is drinkable for people, healthy for aquatic organisms, or suitable for recreation, irrigation, or other uses. Water quality management allows governmental agencies, scientists, and citizens to work toward a mutual goal: keeping water healthy, now and into the future. The Clean Water Act of 1972 delivered this mandate, stating:

> It is the policy of the Congress to recognize, preserve, and protect the primary responsibilities and rights of States to prevent, reduce, and eliminate pollution, [and] to plan the development and use (including restoration, preservation, and enhancement) of land and water resources.

The U.S. Environmental Protection Agency (EPA), established in 1970, was assigned to oversee implementation of the Clean Water Act, supported by agencies in every U.S. jurisdiction.

Two

·Healthy Aquatic Ecosystems

Imagine standing in a valley. Look up at the surrounding hills and you will notice that they all slope in the same direction: toward the floor of the valley. Your valley probably contains a stream or lake. Scientists have a name for this interconnected system of water and land: a watershed. Every spot on Earth is within a watershed. But watersheds do not exist in isolation. They are connected by the flow of water across the landscape. Anything that happens in a watershed has the potential to impact water quality. Even the air and soil are part of this equation, because water also moves through the atmosphere and ground. Human activities may be the most significant factor of all.

Aquatic communities usually occur in the basins of watersheds. Streams and rivers are moving water that flows downslope. Ponds and lakes are standing water located in low points on the landscape. Wetlands are also basins that contain water, though they are typically more shallow, and therefore may spread out rather than growing deeper when water floods in. Saltwater communities have yet different dynamics. Each of these bodies of water is characterized by a different community of organisms and plays a discrete role in the environment.

Wetlands

Due to their shallow basins, wetlands sometimes appear dry. Unless there has been an extended drought, however, water typically lies just below the surface. Apparently "dry" wetlands quickly flood again with a rainfall. The key to identifying wetlands is their characteristic vegetation: tall plants such as cattails, sedges, and bulrushes. These are categorized as "emergent plants," because their roots are immersed in water or mud while their leaves and flowers are in the air. By contrast, submergent plants such as water milfoil manage to grow with all their parts, even leaves, completely underwater. True to their name, floating-leaf plants have leaves that drift on the surface. Water lily is a familiar example. Floating-leaf plants are actually attached to long stems that reach down to the substrate, or bottom sediments, of the wetland. Free-floating plants such as duckweed are not attached to anything. Their roots trail in the water, while the leaves float on the surface.

Dutch colonists in the 1600s were unsure whether to fear or be thrilled by the vast expanses of wetland they found in the region around New York and New Jersey. On the one hand, they considered wetlands unattractive places riddled with disease. On the other hand, drained and filled wetlands made excellent farms. At the time of colonial settlement, the continental United States held 221 million acres (89.4 million hectares) of wetlands. As the population expanded westward in the 1800s, wetlands were filled to create land for farms, as well as for the construction of trails and railroads. Across the nation, more wetlands were filled to make room for ever-growing cities, suburbs, highways, and industries. By the 1980s, fewer than half of the wetlands originally found in the forty-eight contiguous states—only 103 million acres (41.7 million ha)—remained intact. Wetland conversion in California was particularly extensive. Ninety-one percent of that state's wetlands, particularly in the vast Central Valley, are now gone.

A subdivision encroaches upon natural wetlands
in Old Saybrook, Connecticut.

We now know that wetlands play a valuable role in the environment. Whether in freshwater or coastal areas, wetlands provide refuge and nursery sites in which fish lay their eggs and young fish hide from predators. About 138 species of birds native to the United States rely on wetlands either for nesting, feeding, or as stopover sites during long-distance migrations. Wetlands offer direct benefits to humans, as well. They absorb large volumes of water from the surrounding watershed, reducing the impact of flooding. Like sponges, wetlands hold water in place while allowing sediments and potentially harmful nutrients such as nitrogen and phosphorus to settle to the bottom.

The filtration system of wetlands is so effective that scientists have experimented with using wetland plants to treat sewage.

Ponds and Lakes

Ponds and lakes occur wherever earthquakes have caused the ground to sink; in the craters of old volcanoes; where glaciers gouged holes in the land; and in many other low spots. The basin is filled by a combination of precipitation, runoff, flow from incoming streams, and groundwater springs. Water can also exit lakes. Many have outflow streams, and water may percolate through the lake bed into groundwater. Evaporation can also be rapid, especially on warm or windy days.

Several gases are essential for life in aquatic ecosystems. One of the most familiar is oxygen. In lakes, oxygen is stirred into the water by winds that blow over the surface. Living things use oxygen during respiration and in the metabolic breakdown of food to produce energy. Because layers of water—particularly in deep lakes—have different temperatures and densities, water may "turn over" seasonally, with cold lower layers rising and warmer layers falling. This circulates oxygen and other chemicals through the water.

Carbon dioxide and nitrogen also enter water from the air. Plants and algae use carbon dioxide during photosynthesis. Nitrogen makes up more than three-quarters of the atmosphere, and is essential for life. Most organisms, however, cannot use this organic nitrogen gas (N_2). Cyanobacteria (blue-green bacteria) in water "fix," or convert, the nitrogen gas to a soluble solution called nitrate, which can be absorbed by plants. Organisms use forms of nitrogen to build proteins.

Such minerals as phosphorus, iron, sulfur, and carbonate or bicarbonate enter the water, often as a result of erosion. Phosphorus is vital to living things. Like nitrogen, it is used in the production of proteins. It is also the *P* in ATP (*a*denosine *tri*phosphate), which cells use for energy. Nitrogen and phosphorus are called nutrients because they promote growth. Phosphorus is the primary nutrient that controls the rate of plant and algae growth in freshwater ecosystems.

Crater Lake in Oregon is an oligotrophic lake. That is, its depth prevents sediments and nutrients from mixing throughout the water column.

Levels of light, dissolved oxygen (DO), and temperature strongly influence the turbidity of a lake. Turbidity is a measure of how many sediments and nutrients are in a body of water. High levels of nutrients promote the growth of algae, which makes water less clear. There are three categories of lakes, based on the level of nutrients in them and, as a result, their turbidity—oligotrophic, mesotrophic, and eutrophic. Oligotrophic lakes have low levels of nutrients, meaning that they are not very productive and their clarity is high. Deep lakes, such as Crater Lake in Oregon's Cascade Mountains, and Lake Superior, tend to be oligotrophic because their depth prevents turnover—sediments and nutrients from the substrate never get mixed into the column of water. Young lakes are often oligotrophic as well, because it takes time for nutrients to erode into the water. Crater Lake combines both factors. At 1,932 feet (589 m), it is the deepest lake in the United States. It is also a very young lake. Crater Lake sits inside a caldera, or circular crater, that formed just seven thousand years ago after the eruption of Mount Mazama.

Oligotrophic lakes are often clear and lovely to look at, but the lack of nutrients means that they may support a low diversity of plants and animals. Mesotrophic lakes have moderate levels of nutrients. This is an ideal situation: they can support a high diversity of organisms, but do not have so many nutrients that algae can take over. At the far end of the spectrum, eutrophic lakes are overly productive and have very low clarity. Eutrophic lakes may lie in watersheds that have naturally high rates of erosion, or which have very productive soils. Many old lakes are eutrophic as well, because they have had a long time to accumulate sediments and nutrients. Eutrophic lakes may have problems with algae and sometimes experience losses in species diversity because of low clarity.

Many lake organisms are adapted for survival in a particular zone of light, temperature, and oxygen. The benthic zone, at the bottom of the lake, may be very dark and low in oxygen. It is home to bacteria, which decompose the wastes that drift down, along with macroinvertebrates—insect larvae, crustaceans such as crayfish, mollusks (snails), and worms. The open water, or limnetic zone, hosts mostly floating microscopic organisms called plankton. These include photosynthetic organisms that are the primary producers of energy from sunlight, as well as the animal-like zooplankton that consume them. Fish are part of this food web, though they can freely move between the top and bottom layers of water. Along the lakeshore is the littoral zone. There, water is shallow enough that sunlight can penetrate to the bottom. Plant growth is usually lush. As in a wetland, the littoral zone includes emergent, floating-leaf, floating, and submergent vegetation. There is also a myriad of macroinvertebrates. "Macros" are the base of an important food web in the littoral zone, which feeds young fish, frogs, and many other animals.

Streams and Rivers

Streams and rivers are fed by runoff. They may begin as seeps from groundwater springs or as outflow from overflowing

A eutrophic lake is one that has high levels of sediments and nutrients, which promote the growth of algae and aquatic plants.

lakes. Any identifiable beginning place of a stream is called its headwaters. Sometimes streams begin as runoff in steep hills and mountains. Small channels gather into streams, each of which is called a tributary. Tributaries are part of the watershed's drainage basin. Their pattern can be extremely complex, like the branches of a tree. They all flow toward a main body of water in the basin—a lake, large river, or bay.

Along the way, the energy of flowing water erodes the landscape. This process begins on slopes, where runoff occurs. Raindrops loosen particles of soil and rock. Water in sheet flow picks these up and carries them downstream. Erosion takes place on the streambed, as well. The river gradually cuts into the landscape to form its main channel. Moving water easily carries sediments, including silt, sand, and gravel, in the current. Amazingly, water can even move very large boulders. These are too heavy to float; instead, they are transported in tiny jumps along the streambed. Sediments are deposited all along the river's path. Larger pieces are dropped off upstream, forming midstream bars and islands. Small particles remain in the water longest. These are carried along until the river reaches flatlands. Occasional floods also cause the river to overflow its banks; it will then deposit sediments over the surrounding landscape. This water is rich in nutrients. Vegetation alongside rivers is often lush as a result. Even after a flood, a substantial amount of small sediment remains in the river and is carried to the sea.

A riparian zone is a vegetative region that borders a river or other watercourse. A healthy riparian zone contains tall trees as well as shrubs, grasses, and emergent vegetation. This vegetation obtains water and nutrients from the river. In return, tall trees give shade that controls stream temperature. Vegetation holds soil in place, reducing the turbidity of water. Leaves also fall into the water, providing food for macroinvertebrates near the base of the food web. When the riparian zone is removed, water quality in a river quickly declines. A study done in British Columbia, Canada, showed that removing vegetation from the riparian zone around a 5-foot-wide (1.5-m-wide) stream caused its

Unwelcome Visitors

In 1988 a new type of bivalve (two-shelled mollusk) called the zebra mussel (above) was discovered in Lake Saint Clair, Michigan. Scientists identified it as a species normally found in Eastern Europe. They determined that it must have been unintentionally transported to the United States by ships. Ships release any water that is in their holds when they return to port. Organisms in the water—including planktonic organisms such as tiny mussel larvae—are released as well. The environmental impact of such invasive species can be extensive. Zebra mussels grow in large colonies, blocking industrial and wastewater treatment pipes. They also eat voraciously, leaving insufficient food for native mussels. Today, the annual cost for controlling zebra mussels is estimated at $5 billion.

A second invasive mussel, the quagga, was found in Lake Erie in 1989. Both species have spread throughout the Great Lakes and into rivers and lakes in the eastern United States. Zebra and quagga mussels feed by filtering water through their gills and collecting the minute organisms that become captured there. Among other things, the mussels consume a type of bacteria called *Clostridium botulinum*. Most organisms get botulism when they eat this bacterium, which is a deadly form of food poisoning to which both zebra and quagga mussels seem to be immune. Round gobies are not, however. This little fish is another invasive species, and it loves to eat mussels. Unfortunately, there are more than fifty species of native birds that eat round gobies. In 2007 as many as 8,500 birds may have died from botulism on Lake Michigan alone.

The San Pedro River in Cochise, Arizona, has a typical riparian habitat of trees, shrubs, and grasses.

temperature to increase as much as 3.6 degrees Fahrenheit (2 degrees Celsius). Although this number seems small, it can be enough to change the diversity of species that live in the stream. The Canadian study showed that restoring a riparian zone just 33 feet (10 m) wide around the stream prevented temperature changes, even if logging occurred beyond the zone.

In streams, aquatic plants and algae are the primary nutrient producers. Insect macroinvertebrates are another important component of the stream food web. These animals may spend parts of their lives, for example their pupal or adult stages, in the soil or air. During their larval stages, however, they are completely reliant on the stream for their survival.

Saltwater Communities

Saltwater marshes are important ecosystems along many coastlines. Like other wetlands, they are home to diverse organisms, and play an important role in controlling the flow of nutrients that would otherwise enter the ocean from rivers. Plants in these habitats are adapted to deal with salinity changes that come with the tides.

The United States also has 12,380 miles (19,924 km) of coastline that offer diverse habitats. Examples include eelgrass beds, kelp beds, and coral reefs. Eelgrass beds are home to a wide variety of invertebrate animals, including clams, scallops, and sea urchins, as well as many species of fish that are commercially important to people. Kelp beds grow like forests off many shorelines, in water up to 100 feet (30 m) deep. Sunlight floods these regions, allowing the kelp—which is actually a type of alga—to grow to great lengths. Invertebrate larvae float through the "forest," sea urchins feed voraciously on the strands of kelp, and fish hide among them. On the Pacific coast, sea otters make kelp beds their home. They control sea urchin populations and also eat sea stars (starfish), clams, and abalone.

Coral reefs are built by millions of small invertebrate animals called coral polyps. They grow in shallow-water habitats,

Magnificent Macros

When exploring a stream, it is worth looking very closely to find macroinvertebrates. They may be concealed under rocks, among clumps of leaves, around vegetation, or in the muck and mud of the substrate. Stream "macros" are often divided into groups according to their feeding habits: filter feeders, scrapers, shredders, and predators. They are adapted in amazing ways for these lifestyles. The diversity of species found in a stream, and relative numbers of each, is a reflection of water quality. Many macros are extremely sensitive to pollution, and their populations will quickly decline when nutrient levels are too high or dissolved oxygen levels are low.

• Stonefly larvae (above) are large, as macroinvertebrates go: a few species reach a length of 2.8 inches

(71 millimeters). Some are shredders, chewing up leaves and other organic matter. Others are predators. Because these larvae require cool water with a good supply of dissolved oxygen, they are an indicator of very clean water.

- Caddisfly larvae look like tiny caterpillars. Some can spin silk, which they use to make sticky nets to catch food drifting by in the water. Others make cases from the silk. They stick tiny bits of sand, leaves, and twigs all over it, then hide inside. Most caddisflies eat vegetation. Groups range in their pollution tolerance, but none can survive high levels.

- Rat-tailed maggots are the larvae of flower flies. These wormy little creatures have such high tolerance to pollution that they can live in sewage ponds. A long tube extending off the end of the abdomen allows them to obtain oxygen from the air.

A kelp forest grows to great heights in the sunlit waters off the California coast.

usually near coastlines. Polyps obtain calcium from seawater and use it to construct a hard exoskeleton. Because the animals live in huge colonies, they build large, hard structures on the sea floor. Coral reefs are beautifully colored, though coral polyps themselves are white. This is because corals have a symbiotic relationship with algae, which live in their bodies. The algae photosynthesize, giving off oxygen that the corals need for respiration. The corals provide carbon dioxide as a product of respiration, which the algae put to use in photosynthesis. Reefs are like islands in the surrounding ocean. The oxygen produced by corals makes reefs hospitable to a large variety of organisms, and for this reason, coral reefs are often referred to as the rain forests of the ocean. They can also protect coastlines from wave damage by slowing down the force of incoming waves from storms.

Ecosystems Under Threat

Humans have always benefited from aquatic ecosystems. Unfortunately, it appears that our modern way of life is doing them a great deal of harm. Air and water pollution, invasive species, and habitat alteration reduce the diversity of native species in rivers, lakes, wetlands, and oceans. Changes to habitat and species diversity, in turn, alter the various chemical cycles and the global water cycle, and may even play a role in climate change. With this in mind, water quality management has begun to focus on restoring all the functions and diversity of aquatic ecosystems. These systems can then resume benefiting humans and nature, long into the future.

The Clean Water Act

The Clean Water Act of 1972 had a clear

purpose: "to restore and maintain the chemical, physical and biological integrity of the Nation's waters." It clarified that water pollution has many sources, and placed these into two broad categories: point and nonpoint sources. Point source pollution is conveyed directly into water through pipes, ditches, or tunnels, or is leaked through containers such as ships, as in the case of an oil spill. It can therefore be traced back to a particular location, or "point." Common point sources are factories, sewage and wastewater treatment plants, animal feeding operations (AFOs, where large groups of livestock and poultry are raised), construction sites, and mines. Stormwater pipes were identified as point sources in later amendments to the act.

According to the U.S. EPA, nonpoint source pollution:

> comes from many diffuse sources. NPS pollution is caused by rainfall or snowmelt moving over and through the ground. As the runoff moves, it picks up and carries away natural and human-made pollutants,

This outflow pipe from a chemical factory is a good example of point source pollution.

finally depositing them into lakes, rivers, wetlands, coastal waters, and even our underground sources of drinking water. These pollutants include:

- Excess fertilizers, herbicides, and insecticides from agricultural lands and residential areas;

- Oil, grease, and toxic chemicals from urban runoff and energy production;

- Sediment from improperly managed construction sites, crop and forest lands, and eroding streambanks;

37

- Salt from irrigation practices and acid drainage from abandoned mines;

- Bacteria and nutrients from livestock, pet wastes, and faulty septic systems.

Atmospheric deposition and hydromodification are also sources of nonpoint source pollution.

Seven goals and policies were outlined in the Clean Water Act to deal with these sources of pollution and promote the overall goal of "chemical, physical and biological integrity":

- Pollution discharges into water sources would be eliminated by 1985.

- By 1983 bodies of water would be safe for fishing, swimming, and drinking.

- All toxic pollutants would be limited to small discharge amounts to prevent their harmful effects.

- Federal funding would be made available to build more wastewater treatment plants.

- Every state would develop plans to control its pollution sources.

- New technology would be developed and applied to control pollutants.

- Programs would be implemented to control both point and nonpoint sources of pollution.

The U.S. EPA was assigned to oversee implementation of the legislation. All legal jurisdictions in the United States—states, American-Indian lands, the District of Columbia, and U.S. territories, such as Puerto Rico and American Samoa—were expected to fulfill the requirements of the act within their boundaries. They could do this through their own state agencies or ask the EPA to supervise.

Water pollution control efforts would now reach beyond just identifying sources and protecting human health. The Clean Water Act sought to return aquatic systems to a natural state—and to keep them healthy.

Water Quality Standards

The Clean Water Act (CWA) consists of many sections, each of which outlines requirements to help fulfill the seven primary goals. Section 303 of the original Clean Water Act of 1972 required the first action from jurisdictions, demanding that they evaluate the wetlands, streams, rivers, ponds, lakes, and bays within their boundaries. Based on their findings, each jurisdiction (which are collectively referred to as "states") would prepare water quality standards. These consist of three components: designated uses, water quality criteria, and antidegradation policy.

Each body of water is unique, affected by different environmental and land-use factors. Standards for maintaining, or improving, water quality must therefore be developed on a case-by-case basis. Designated uses are the human and wildlife uses, and ecological functions, a body of water could support if its quality were high. Section 303(c) names several categories of designated uses, including "public water supplies, propagation of fish and wildlife, recreational purposes, and agricultural, industrial, and other purposes, and also taking into consideration their use and value for navigation." The designated uses for Utah's Great Salt Lake, for example, include recreation (swimming and boating), wildlife habitat, and mineral extraction. The Columbia River in Washington and Oregon is designated for water supply, industry, irrigation, livestock watering, fish and wildlife, recreation, aesthetic beauty, hydropower, and navigation. In the long run, poor water quality often prevents designated uses from being fulfilled. "Existing uses" provide a more accurate reflection of reality. These take three forms: (1) uses that are currently taking place on a body of water, (2) uses that have taken place since 1975 (whether current or not), or (3) uses that have been made possible because of improvements in water

quality (even if these uses are not currently occurring). Existing uses are also protected by the act.

The second stage of water quality standard development involves setting criteria. These criteria explain how designated uses will be protected, or establish goals to achieve them. States are required to set water quality criteria that limit the concentrations of toxic pollutants. Pollutants are measured according to numeric—quantitative—criteria. Numeric criteria are also used to limit specific ranges of pH (acidity and alkalinity), dissolved oxygen, temperature, and other chemical, physical, and biological aspects of water quality. Criteria can also be qualitative, describing desirable conditions. These include statements such as "able to support a diverse population of aquatic organisms" or "free of nutrients in concentrations that may cause algal blooms."

Finally, water quality standards require the development of antidegradation policies. Antidegradation is a kind of maintenance program. Its role is to prevent or reduce activities that could cause deterioration of water quality. All projects that impact water must be evaluated. They can be rejected, or required to undergo revision, if the quality of receiving waters will be compromised. Currently, antidegradation efforts focus heavily on protection of wetlands, flood control, and reduction of stormwater runoff, because these have all been shown to contribute to the decline of aquatic habitats and water quality.

State agencies are closely involved in antidegradation work. Departments of natural resources, fish and wildlife departments, soil and water conservation districts, and pollution control agencies can have a significant impact by working with citizens, industries, and municipalities (towns, cities, and counties) to reduce their impact on water quality. The best antidegradation work is often done at the local level. Some states have watershed districts to aid in this process. These are organizations that manage water within a single watershed region. Watershed boundaries are not usually the same as political boundaries. Watershed districts can coordinate decision making between cities and counties. They may issue permits to ensure responsible development and often provide important public education.

40

In order to monitor for PCB levels in the upper Hudson River, a New York State environmental engineer takes water samples.

Tracking Water Quality

The Clean Water Act requires that states monitor water quality to ensure that standards are being met. Data from monitoring can help identify types and sources of pollution. They aid in the development of prevention programs, and reveal whether management plans are effective. Data are also important to keep the public informed about the conditions of local waters.

There are two types of monitoring—compliance and ambient. Compliance monitoring checks the effluent discharges from permitted point source polluters, such as sewage treatment plants and factories. Toxic chemicals, heavy metals, fecal coliform bacteria, and nutrients may be tested at these sites. Ambient monitoring determines the physical, biological, and chemical conditions of bodies of water. A thorough survey includes four components: habitat assessment (nearby land use and physical condition of the water body), physical testing (temperature, turbidity, and flow rate or water level), chemical testing (pH, dissolved oxygen, and nutrients—phosphorus and nitrogen—and sometimes alkalinity or chlorides), as well as biomonitoring of stream organisms.

Implementing the Act

The primary goal of the Clean Water Act of 1972 was to prevent point source pollution. The law states that "the discharge of any pollutant by any person shall be unlawful." Factories and sewage plants were now regulated. These sources produce effluents, which are liquid waste discharges. Prior to the CWA, effluents were routinely dumped into bodies of water, with few controls placed on the level of toxins allowed. The Clean Water Act changed this. It required point source polluters to use the best technology available to meet state water quality standards, and mandated that all polluters obtain a permit before releasing effluents.

Section 402 of the CWA—more commonly known as the National Pollutant Discharge Elimination System (NPDES)—defines the criteria for obtaining an effluent discharge permit. States can apply for the option to oversee their own permits or

Water Quality Monitoring

When it's time to monitor water quality, the following are the physical, chemical, and biological surveys most commonly conducted.

Physical

- Temperature determines the amount of dissolved oxygen (DO) that water can hold: warmer water holds less DO.

- Turbidity is dependent on the number of suspended particles (sediment, organic material, or algae). High turbidity reduces clarity. Suspended materials absorb light, making less light available for plants and increasing the water temperature—which in turn reduces DO.

- The amount of water moving past a point in a certain amount of time is flow rate. It varies depending on stream structure, and changes rapidly during rainfall. Impervious surfaces cause flow rates to increase rapidly after rainfall, which can lead to erosion and sedimentation. In lakes, water level affects clarity.

Chemical

- The acidity of water is measured by pH. Literally, it is the concentration of hydrogen ions dissolved in the water. Atmospheric pollutants such as sulphur dioxide and CO_2 have a strong influence on pH.

(continued)

- DO is the oxygen available for aquatic organisms to breathe. DO increases in cooler water.

- Although used for growth and energy, high levels of phosphorus cause overgrowth of algae (eutrophication) in freshwater habitats. Phosphorus pollution generally comes from manure and fertilizers or from wastewater that is not treated well for detergents and cleaning solutions.

- Nitrogen, another nutrient, has many sources. Sewage and fertilizers are the top culprits. Nitrogen causes eutrophication in saltwater.

Biological

- Macroinvertebrates have specific tolerances to water pollution. Their diversity and population sizes in a body of water can be good indicators of water quality, even if other tests are inconclusive.

ask the EPA to do it for them. Two categories of NPDES permits are granted: those for individual sites (such as a specific factory or animal feeding operation) and those that cover a range of similar discharges in the same region (for example, all the stormwater drains in a city).

Each permit applicant must show exactly which pollutants are being discharged and where. The permit determines the level of each pollutant that is safe to discharge. This varies based on the standards applied to the body of water receiving the pollutants. Permits also establish how often water must be monitored. Because local citizens are impacted by changes in

Section 402 of the Clean Water Act outlines information for manufacturing plants pertaining to their discharging of pollutants into the environment. This effluent is emanating from a sugarcane refinery in Louisiana.

water use, new permits are always made available to the public for comment. They must also be renewed every five years. In addition to permits, each industry must meet particular standards for treating effluents before discharging them into water bodies or stormwater runoff. According to the U.S. EPA's 2006 Toxics Release Inventory report, 4.25 billion pounds (1.9 billion kilograms) of toxic chemicals were released from almost 23,000 facilities that have permits with the EPA.

Permits are also required for dredging and filling. This is a process by which mud, dirt, and other materials are moved into and out of wetlands, streams, and lakes. Dredging is commonly done to keep shipping channels open; many industrial construction projects also move sediments. Minimal disturbance to sediments is important, because they often contain high levels of pollutants. Dredge and Fill permits are administered under Section 404 of the Clean Water Act. These permits are issued exclusively by the Army Corps of Engineers, which

This dredging vessel sucks water and silt off Key West, Florida, in an effort to clear a cruise ship channel.

is responsible for navigation, flood control, disaster response, and any construction that occurs on "navigable waters of the United States." These are defined as bodies of water large enough to be used for navigation between states, or that flow into such waters.

Reporting the Results

Section 305(b) originally required each state to monitor its waters and provide comprehensive reports every other year. A regular reporting cycle is important to ensure that state waters are fulfilling their designated uses and to determine whether there are trends in water quality improvement or decline. Results are compiled in a federal report called the National Water Quality Inventory (NWQI). The two-year cycle was problematic because it did not give states enough time to monitor all of their waters. As of 1996 the U.S. EPA advocated a new approach. States now have five years to complete their 305(b) reports—but in that time, they are expected to monitor all bodies of water within their jurisdictions. Yearly progress reports are also expected so the EPA and the public can remain informed between NWQI reports.

States must also prepare a Section 303(d) list of Threatened and Impaired Waters. These are waters that fail to meet one or more water quality standards. A specific plan must be drawn up for each body of water on the Section 303(d) list, detailing how water quality standards will be achieved. Whether the source of impairment is a toxic pollutant coming from a point source, nutrients that result from nonpoint source pollution, or some other factor, goals must be set up to control the problem. These plans are called Total Maximum Daily Loads (TMDLs). TMDLs include numeric limits for discharge of each pollutant. They also describe methods for reducing discharges from each source.

The Water Quality Act of 1987

The Water Quality Act of 1987 amended the Clean Water Act in several important ways. Its main focus was to control nonpoint source (NPS) pollution. A new section of the act, Section 319, laid out a three-point plan:

1. Determine which waters are impacted by NPS pollution.

2. Identify categories of pollution.

3. Develop management plans to address any problems that were identified.

These plans include a time line for improvement and a list of best management practices (BMPs)—methods that can be used by scientists, businesses, and industries to reduce nonpoint source pollution. The EPA is responsible for approving state NPS reduction plans. Once approved, states are eligible to apply for federal grants to help fund their programs.

Section 319 dictates that "a State shall, to the maximum extent practical, develop and implement a manageable program

under this subsection on a watershed-by-watershed basis within such State." For the first time, states were actively encouraged to look at the collective forces that might be impacting watersheds, so they could treat them holistically rather than dealing with individual point sources.

Another vital aspect of the Water Quality Act of 1987 was its treatment of stormwater (runoff) pollution. Point sources had originally been defined as those that transport pollutants in any "pipe, ditch, channel, tunnel, conduit, well, [or] discrete fissure." This definition was thereafter applied to stormwater pollution (although it was not extended to cover runoff from agricultural fields). Control of stormwater runoff was implemented in two phases. Phase I required larger sources of stormwater runoff to obtain NPDES permits by 1992. These include:

- construction sites larger than 5 acres

- industries that produce stormwater

- cities with populations greater than 100,000 that use municipal separate storm sewer systems (MS4s)

MS4s consist of two separate sets of piping: one for stormwater and a second, called a sanitary sewer, to carry waste from homes and industries. In cities with MS4s, sanitary sewage is treated before being released into bodies of water. Prior to Phase I, stormwater pipes often discharged directly into water. Large MS4s were now required to obtain NPDES permits and to treat this stormwater. The nation's other form of public sewage system, called a combined sewer (CSS), carries both sanitary waste and stormwater in the same pipes. CSSs are not required to have NPDES permits because they lead to wastewater treatment plants. They are not perfect, however, and sometimes overflow.

Phase II was delayed somewhat, and did not go into effect until 2003. It requires permits for small MS4s. These typically serve communities smaller than 50,000, as well as campuses such as those used by the military, governmental offices, universities, hospitals, and prisons. Smaller construction projects that disturb blocks of land 1 to 4 acres (0.4 to 1.6 ha) in size also require Phase II permits.

Drinking Water Safety

The Clean Water Act is intended to improve water quality for many uses. Given the number of pollutants in water, and the recurrent risk of waterborne diseases, Congress chose to pass additional legislation regulating the safety of drinking water. The Safe Drinking Water Act of 1974 (SDWA) allowed the U.S. EPA to set standards for drinking water supplies. States and local water providers work with the EPA to fulfill those standards.

In its 1990 census, the U.S. Census Bureau included questions about the types of sewer and water systems used by Americans. The results reveal that approximately 85 percent of Americans obtain their drinking water through public water systems—those serving at least twenty-five people, for sixty days or more during the year. Private wells provide water for most everyone else. In 2007 there were 156,000 public drinking water systems in the nation: 52,000 in cities and towns, and the remainder in schools, office buildings, hospitals, campgrounds, and other public locations that offer water. In U.S. public water systems, roughly 68 percent of drinking water comes from surface water sources. The proportion accessed from groundwater increases among rural populations.

Drinking water can never be made absolutely "pure"—if it were, it would be flavorless. There is an important distinction between minerals that give water flavor and contaminants that may harm human health or wildlife. Both surface and groundwater can be threatened by a wide variety of pollutants that come from natural as well as point and nonpoint sources. Erosion of rocks can release some hazardous particles, such as arsenic and radionuclides (radioactive particles that can result from erosion). Pesticides, herbicides, and fungicides are inorganic and organic chemicals commonly used on farms, in gardens, and on public green spaces such as golf courses.

They may run off or infiltrate into soil. Landfills are another significant source of groundwater pollution. These often contain discarded batteries, cleaning solutions, paint, and other sources of chemicals or heavy metals. Some landfills have liners that prevent infiltration. Others do not, which permits those toxins to enter groundwater. Surface impoundments such as reservoirs or other places where water is trapped are equally dangerous. In these basins, wastes such as stormwater, sewage, manure, or other liquids are left to settle so pollutants can descend to the bottom. If the reservoir or basin is poorly constructed, the pollutants can leach into groundwater. Mining, leaks and spills from industrial activities, underground storage tanks (such as those used to hold fuels at gas stations), and underground septic tanks that hold sewage are other sources of groundwater pollution.

The SDWA requires that drinking water be protected from contamination in a variety of ways. Maximum contaminant levels (MCLs) are limits set on the concentrations of

Passed in 1974, the Safe Drinking Water Act sets national standards for the health of drinking water supplies.

pollutants in drinking water. As of 2008 the EPA had set MCLs on approximately ninety substances. Next, water must be treated to remove contaminants that are present. Some regions have source waters that are very clean, requiring only disinfection to reduce the risk of pathogens. Other areas have water that is highly turbid. These need more intensive treatment, involving filtration, flocculation, sedimentation, and disinfection. Flocculation is the use of gel-like substances that cause particles to clump into loosely organized larger bundles. Fluoride is often added to water as a final touch; when used in small amounts, it can prevent tooth decay.

In 1986 and 1996 amendments to the SDWA required that drinking-water providers include pollution prevention and public education in their programs. Prevention requires that states and drinking-water providers must regularly check water supplies for possible sources of pollution. The public must be informed of any failures in a water treatment system. Suppliers are also expected to provide education on drinking-water safety. Consumers should receive a yearly report that describes the quality of source waters in their region and discusses how their water supplier has handled treatment and any problems.

Where Do We Stand Today?

In October 2007 the latest National Water Quality Inventory was published. It contained Section 305(b) water quality reports conducted by the states through 2002. For the first time, some states submitted these reports in combination with Section 303(d) lists of Threatened and Impaired Waters.

The NWQI indicates that about 30 percent of all U.S. waters were assessed during the 2002 reporting cycle. The outcomes are not encouraging. According to the U.S. EPA, "about 45% of assessed stream miles, 47% of assessed lake acres, and 32% of bay and estuarine square miles were not clean enough to support uses such as fishing and swimming." The main causes of impairment for U.S. waters are listed as excess levels of nutrients, metals (especially mercury),

Group of Waters	Rivers and Streams
Table 1. Causes and Sources of Pollution in U.S. Waters	
Total in U.S.	3.7 million miles (5.95 million km)
Percent Assessed	19%
Major Causes of Pollution	Sediments Pathogens Habitat alteration
Primary Sources of Pollution	Agricultural activities Unknown sources Hydrological modifications (diversion and channelization)

Lakes, Ponds, and Reservoirs	Bays and Estuaries
40.6 million acres (16.4 million ha)	87,369 acres (35,358 ha)
37%	35%
Nutrients Metals Organic enrichment/ low dissolved oxygen	Metals Nutrients Organic enrichment/ low dissolved oxygen
Unknown sources Agricultural activities Atmospheric deposition	Unknown sources Industry Municipal discharges (especially from sewage treatment plants)

Source: The National Water Quality Inventory: Report to Congress for the 2002 Reporting Cycle.

A Quick Look at Environmental Legislation

A variety of federal laws have been passed in the past half-century to address various aspects of environmental health. Many of these relate to water quality. Use your library or your favorite search engine to learn about these and other environmental laws. Search "EPA laws."

- Title IV of the Civil Rights Act of 1964

- Federal Insecticide, Fungicide, and Rodenticide Act of 1947 (FIFRA)

- National Wild and Scenic Rivers Act of 1968 (WSRA)

- Clean Air Act of 1970 (CAA)

- National Environmental Policy Act of 1970 (NEPA)

- Coastal Zone Management Act of 1972 (CZMA)

- Marine Protection, Research and Sanctuaries Act of 1972 (MPRSA, or "Ocean Dumping Act")

- Toxic Substances Control Act of 1976 (TSCA)

- Comprehensive Environmental Response, Compensation, and Liability Act of 1980 (CERCLA, "Superfund")

- Oil Pollution Act of 1990 (OPA)

- Farm Security and Rural Investment Act of 2002 (FSRIA, the "Farm Bill")

sediment and organic enrichment (high levels of algae that deplete oxygen in the water). These pollutants come primarily from:

- agriculture: irrigated and nonirrigated crops, grazing and ranching, and animal feeding operations
- hydrological modification: creating channels, diverting water (as for irrigation), damming, and dredging
- atmospheric deposition: acid precipitation and fallout of dry particles from air to ground
- industry
- unknown or unspecified sources (probably nonpoint sources such as urban runoff and municipal water treatment).

Four

Our Impact on Water

Permeable soils allow water to percolate slowly into groundwater. Soils can remove some pollutants, and they promote the growth of healthy vegetation, which in turn reduces soil erosion. Studies show that in areas with natural, largely undisturbed soil and forest, approximately 35 percent of precipitation percolates into groundwater, while only 15 percent runs off—just enough to replenish bodies of surface water but not to flood or erode them.

Human land use alters these natural patterns of infiltration and runoff. Urban land use, in cities and industrial areas, often replaces natural landscapes with impervious surfaces—roads, parking lots, rooftops, and other solid surfaces that cannot absorb water. Water quickly runs off them. In suburban areas, land cover averages about four houses per acre (0.4 ha) of land. (One acre is slightly smaller than a U.S. football field.) This creates about 35 percent impervious surface. At this level of land use, only about 16 percent of water can infiltrate, while 70 percent may run off. The health of streams is impacted by just 10 percent of impervious surface; 25 percent of impervious surface in a watershed can cause

When undeveloped land is replaced with industrial areas, roads, and housing developments, for example, water is not capable of percolation and becomes runoff.

severe degradation to the point that fewer species can survive and the water becomes unhealthy for human use. In locations where impervious surface is 100 percent, no infiltration takes place. More than 80 percent of precipitation runs off, and the rest evaporates. Many cities and industrial sites have very high levels of impervious surface.

Impervious surfaces degrade water in a variety of ways. They cause runoff to enter streams very quickly, promoting erosion and, sometimes, flooding. Runoff picks up any materials lying on top of impervious surfaces: oil and gas, decaying leaves, pet and bird waste, road salts used for de-icing, and more. Temperature changes can also occur. For example, the temperature on a gravel roof in summer can be 140 to 176 °F (60 to 80 °C). Heat is transferred to runoff water as it passes over such surfaces; the heat is then added to streams and lakes when runoff pours into them through storm sewers. Warm water holds less oxygen. It also slows down the metabolism of organisms such as trout

that are adapted for cold water. Most aquatic organisms can adjust to seasonal shifts in water temperature, but do not tolerate rapid changes. After a summer rainstorm in 2001, 184 trout were found dead along a 1.5-mile (2.4-km) stretch of McLoud Run, a stream that flows through Cedar Rapids, Iowa. McLoud Run is the only urban stream in Iowa with conditions that can support these popular and ecologically important fish. There are countless locations around the nation suffering similar problems.

Sediments, Nutrients, and Chemicals
Sediment comes from farm fields, construction sites, roadways, and other areas that have been stripped of vegetation. A study at the University of Idaho found that erosion carries about 5 million tons (4.5 million metric tons) of sediment a year into that state's water; as previously mentioned, the worldwide annual total is 4 billion tons (3.6 billion metric tons). The rate of erosion varies depending on slope, the amount of vegetation on the land, and other factors. Floating sediment degrades the quality of drinking water. Sediments also can be harmful to organisms, for example by clogging fish gills, burying fish nests on stream and lake beds, blocking light to submergent plants, and changing water temperature.

Layers of sediment can also hold large amounts of toxic chemicals, which enter water through runoff, in industrial discharges, or by atmospheric deposition. Chemicals may remain in sediments for years. San Francisco Bay is one of the nation's largest and richest estuaries, where freshwater from rivers mixes with saline water from the ocean. Sadly, sediments on the floor of the bay are badly contaminated by industrial and agricultural chemicals. Some of the pollutants in the bay sediments include the insecticide dichloro-diphenyl-trichloroethane (DDT), mercury, arsenic, polychlorinated biphenyls (PCBs), and polycyclic aromatic hydrocarbons (PAHs). Many of these chemicals are absorbed into the bodies of benthic (bottom-dwelling) animals as they feed, then move up through the food chain to harm animals and humans alike (see Table 2).

Table 2. **Chemical Pollutants in San Francisco Bay Sediments**

Pollutant	Description; Source in San Francisco Bay sediments
DDT	A pesticide that was first used to control mosquitoes in World War II, DDT was later put into wide use as an agricultural insecticide. It was eventually linked to declines in many bird populations and suggested as a risk for cancer among humans. It was banned in 1972 but has a long half-life. DDT continues to show up in sediments in several forms.
Mercury	Historically used in gold mining, this chemical element is also released during fossil fuel combustion and industrial processes. It is carried in the air and deposited into water. Health risks include neurological delays and kidney disease.
Arsenic	A natural chemical element that may occur in groundwater-containing rocks, arsenic is also produced through mining or industrial activity and is a component of some pesticides. Prolonged exposure can lead to a variety of forms of cancer.

(continued)

Table 2. Chemical Pollutants in San Francisco Bay Sediments

Pollutant	Description; Source in San Francisco Bay sediments
Polychlorinated biphenyls (PCBs)	Man-made chemicals first used in the 1920s as coolants and lubricants for industry. They were banned in 1978 due to health risks. Like mercury, PCBs bioaccumulate through the food web. Humans are exposed by eating contaminated animals.
Polycyclic aromatic hydrocarbons (PAHs)	PAHs occur naturally in fossil fuels and are released when these are burned. Cancer and risks to reproduction and development can result from exposure. Humans and animals are exposed to PAH by bioaccumulation.

Fertilizers, pesticides, fungicides, and herbicides are among the most challenging sources of pollution to prevent, because they are used so widely—not only on agricultural fields, but also on large turf areas such as golf courses and in yards of homes. Many of these chemicals show up in surface and groundwater and can persist in sediments for long periods. Pesticides are used to kill insects that eat plants. Forms of pesticides have been in use for centuries, but they came into widespread use with the development of DDT in the 1940s during World War II. DDT was found to eliminate a wide variety of insect pests. Unfortunately, it also is able to last a long time in the environment, causing a myriad

Pesticides sprayed on crops are one source of pollution that can appear in surface and groundwater.

of negative effects along the way. Populations of large birds, such as the bald eagle, began to decline as the chemical accumulated in their bodies. DDT was banned in 1972, but many other pesticides soon took its place. In 2000 pesticide use in the United States totaled more than 1.2 billion pounds (0.5 billion kg).

Herbicides are used to kill unwanted plants. Glyphosate, a commonly used organophosphate herbicide, was found

61

in 39 percent of fifty-one Midwestern streams studied by the U.S. Geological Survey in 2002. Its chemical by-products (products created as glyphosate breaks down in the environment) were found in 69 percent of the streams. Another herbicide, atrazine, was also identified in some of the streams. Although the glyphosate samples were all within the ranges set by the U.S. EPA for safe drinking water, 30 percent of the streams showed atrazine levels at or above EPA limits. Atrazine has been associated with hormonal changes in male frogs, and the Centers for Disease Control cautions that it may cause reproductive problems in human females, including premature births. Due to concerns for human and environmental health, agricultural chemicals are monitored by the EPA under the 1947 Federal Insecticide, Fungicide, and Rodenticide Act. This legislation requires all pesticides, whether made in the United States or imported, to be registered and then reviewed for safety every five years.

Nutrients have perhaps been the most harmful to aquatic ecosystems. They enter water from fertilizers—chemicals used to increase the rate of growth in plants—or from animal wastes. Manure was the first fertilizer applied by man and is still used today. Sewage sludge is often spread on agricultural fields as well. Chemical fertilizers contain high levels of synthetic nitrogen and phosphorus. Plants absorb some of these nutrients, which are then passed on to people or animals that consume the food. Nitrogen and phosphorus may also be held in soil, but a substantial amount of nutrients are lost to the environment.

Phosphorus is considered a limiting factor in freshwater ecosystems—its availability controls the rate of growth in freshwater plants and algae. Nitrogen limits growth in saltwater habitats. High levels of these nutrients cause algae to "bloom," growing rapidly until they may cover an area of the water's surface. As algae die, they create a food source for bacteria. Large bacterial populations use most of the oxygen in the water, which results in zones of low or zero oxygen in the water, called hypoxic zones. Fish and other aquatic organisms require dissolved oxygen to survive, just as organisms on land breathe oxygen from the air. Under hypoxic conditions,

This satellite image of the "Dead Zone" in the Gulf of Mexico shows the red and orange areas that represent high concentrations of algae and other plankton and river sediment extending from the mouth of the Mississippi River.

the diversity in aquatic ecosystems declines. The food web is impacted; the fishing industry often suffers as well. Since 1985 scientists have been observing a hypoxic zone that formed on the Louisiana coast, where the Mississippi River discharges into the Gulf of Mexico. Between 2003 and 2007, the average size of the Gulf hypoxic zone was 4,200 square miles (10,878 square km). It is caused primarily by nitrogen runoff from agriculture and stormwater.

Sewage and stormwater runoff from animal feeding operations (AFOs) are another significant source of nutrients in water. AFOs are enclosures where meat and dairy animals are maintained. Typically, AFOs contain large numbers of animals in small spaces. The result is a large volume of manure: 500 million tons (454 million metric tons) per year nationwide. Most AFOs have moderate numbers of animals—but a few are

The Chesapeake Bay

The Chesapeake Bay is a 64,000-square-mile (165,760-square-km) watershed that drains from six states in the eastern United States. With thousands of miles of coastline, it has long been an inviting destination for people as well as for wildlife. But population increases and ever-more-dense land use in the watershed over the past fifty years have taken their toll. A study conducted by *National Geographic* in 2005 reported daunting statistics. The region is home to more than 16 million people. In the ten-year period from 1995 to 2005, impervious surfaces increased by 41 percent, while native habitats declined. Agriculture is also an important element of the region's economy and culture. In 2005 nitrogen levels were reported to be sixteen times higher than those that would have been found at the time of colonization in the 1600s; phosphorus levels were thirty times higher. As a result of these influences, each year brings blooms of algae in many parts of the bay, along with declines in such valuable native species as crabs and oysters.

In 1983 a report ordered by Congress revealed that Chesapeake Bay suffered from high nutrient levels and toxic pollution, overharvesting of aquatic wildlife, and loss of sea grass beds. In response, a partnership was made among three of the states—Pennsylvania, Maryland, and Virginia—the District of Columbia, the EPA, and the Chesapeake Bay Commission. The Chesapeake Bay Agreement set goals to "oversee the implementation of coordinated plans to improve and protect the water quality and living resources of the Chesapeake Bay estuarine systems."

Pennsylvania has made strides by requiring wastewater treatment plants to significantly reduce nutrients in their effluents, and by offering incentives to farmers for actions that reduce runoff and sedimentation. Between 2004 and 2006 the state's contributions of nitrogen, phosphorus, and sediment to Chesapeake Bay fell noticeably. Progress is slow, and time alone will tell if the great watershed will recover.

extremely large. Four percent of AFOs in the United States have so many animals that they produce more than 60 percent of the manure.

Sewage Pollution

Human sewage was recognized as a pollutant early in the nineteenth century. Philadelphia, Chicago, and New York were among the first cities to do something about this problem. In the mid–1800s these cities put in combined sewer (CSS) tunnels under every street. Each household, business, and factory was required to build a connection to the system. In these early sewer systems, pipes diverted sewage into local rivers and lakes.

At the time, it was believed that water could dilute and, eventually, purify pollutants. Before long, this theory proved wrong. By the 1870s sewage pollution had caused declines in the productivity of oyster beds in coastal bays, such as those around New York City. Bacteria levels in the Hudson River, which flows into New York's harbor, were measured at 170 times safe levels. Sewage piped into Lake Erie (one of the five Great Lakes) from the cities of Buffalo, Toledo, and Cleveland had created hypoxic zones as early as 1909.

Sewage pollution can also lead to illness. In early 1906, 2,300 people in Philadelphia were infected by typhoid, a sometimes-fatal bacterial infection with symptoms similar to severe food poisoning. A London physician, Dr. John Snow, had discovered in 1848 that typhoid is carried in water. He traced one outbreak of the disease to a house in the Soho district of that city. The house's cesspool was leaking into the local water supply. When local people stopped drinking from the well near that house, they stopped getting sick. Britain set up systems to filter its drinking water supplies soon thereafter, but it would be decades before water filtration became accepted in the United States. Meanwhile, thousands of people each year became ill from typhoid, cholera, and other pathogens (disease-causing organisms) carried in sewage.

Philadelphia dealt with this problem in 1909 by opening a water treatment plant. All of its CSS pipes were diverted there. Four years later, that plant added chlorine treatment to kill pathogens. Many cities built combined sewer systems in the late 1800s and early 1900s. Some later chose to install MS4 systems, with one set of pipes taking sanitary sewage to a treatment plant and another set diverting stormwater to bodies of water.

Both systems present problems. For decades, MS4s allowed stormwater to go untreated. Although amendments to the Clean Water Act in 1987 required larger MS4s to provide stormwater treatment, small MS4 systems can still send stormwater directly into waterways. Additionally, many CSSs are designed to divert sewage into local waterways if the pipes become too full. This keeps treatment plants from becoming overwhelmed during storms, but can be very damaging to the health of water.

Combined sewer systems serve approximately 46 million people in 836 U.S. cities. Overflows from these, and untreated sewage from small MS4s, is a primary cause of pollution along coastlines. Around the United States—from California to Hawaii, the Gulf Coast to New Jersey, and even along the Great Lakes—outbreaks of harmful bacteria from sewage have forced local officials to close beaches. In 2004, for example, there were almost 20,000 health advisories and beach closings. Many of the materials in sewage—especially feces, fertilizers, and detergents—also contain high levels of nutrients that contribute to eutrophication (overgrowth of algae).

Fecal coliform bacteria in water provide evidence of sewage pollution. These are commonly found in the digestive systems of mammals—including humans and livestock. Most are not dangerous, though a few can cause gastroenteritis, a short-term (but still uncomfortable) intestinal illness. The real concern is that feces contamination brings along pathogens and nutrients. Pathogens include viruses, other bacteria, and protozoa (single-celled organisms) such as *Giardia* and *Cryptosporidium.* When people drink water containing these pathogens, serious infections or even death can result. To ensure that prevention and treatment

Modern Wastewater Treatment

American wastewater treatment plants come in all sizes—from small local plants to Chicago's colossal Stickney Water Reclamation Plant, where 1.2 billion gallons (4.5 billion L) of sewage are processed each year. Whatever their size, all sewage treatment plants first use primary treatment. Incoming sewage is called influent. Filters remove large items such as sand and dirt, trash, and food. Wastewater then settles. Heavy particles sink to the bottom; oily materials float and can be skimmed from the surface. Gummy substances called flocculants may also be added. Solid particles in the water cling to them and clump together. Unfortunately, detergents (a source of phosphorus) and pathogens may pass through this process unaffected.

Since 1972 secondary treatment has been required of all municipal (town and city) water treatment plants. This treatment exposes wastewater to bacteria. In the presence of oxygen, these bacteria can consume pathogens and break down detergents. Two products result from secondary treatment: treated effluent that is disposed of into bodies of water (oceans, lakes, rivers, lagoons), and sludge. Sludge is a solid material that is usually further broken down by bacteria. The remaining material should not be returned to waterways—it is burned, sent to a landfill, or used as fertilizer. The goal of secondary treatment is to remove

85 percent of organic materials in wastewater before it is released as effluent.

Today, some plants add tertiary, or third-level, treatment so that water is sufficiently clean for drinking. These treatment plants have the capacity to produce reclaimed water that can be used for irrigating nonedible plants. Many systems use chlorine or other disinfectants to kill pathogens; others apply ultraviolet (UV) light or ozone to accomplish this goal. Phosphorus, nitrogen, and heavy metals can be removed during tertiary treatment as well. Tertiary treatment seeks to leave the outgoing water, called effluent, 95 percent free of contaminants.

systems are working, the U.S. EPA requires drinking water treatment plants to sample water many times each month. If more than five samples per month show positive results for coliform (meaning that the bacteria are present), the plant must notify the public and step up its treatment efforts. Chlorine will usually kill *Giardia*. But *Cryptosporidium* is much more difficult to remove, and is best prevented by stopping runoff containing animal wastes from entering water supplies.

As of 1988 almost 10 percent of Americans were connected to smaller sewer systems that provided only primary treatment—or no treatment at all. About one in four Americans lives in rural locations where homes have no connection to sewage systems. Instead, sewage is treated in private septic systems. Septic systems are underground storage tanks that should provide effective primary wastewater treatment. Nonetheless, when they are not maintained, they can leak sewage into groundwater supplies, tainting them with coliform and associated pathogens, phosphorus, and other chemicals. The Blue Earth River watershed basin in southern Minnesota is representative of this problem. The basin has about 14,000 homes with private septic systems— 40 percent of which did not meet state standards in 2005. Many people are not even aware of the need to maintain their septic systems.

Airborne Pollution
Pollutants in the air come primarily from fossil fuels burned in vehicles and coal power plants. Sulfur dioxide (SO_2) and nitrogen oxides (NO_x) result from this combustion. These gases react with water and oxygen in the atmosphere to form sulfuric acid and nitric acid, then fall back to earth in precipitation or as dry particles. Acids like these can change the pH of wetlands, rivers, and lakes. In the presence of acids, aquatic organisms may experience reproductive abnormalities, as well as reductions in their ability to take in oxygen. Sulfuric acid can also cause heavy metals, such as aluminum and mercury, to be released from soils and rocks into the watershed.

Mills in Indiana pollute the air with emissions from coal-powered generators.

Gases containing carbon, chlorine, and sulfur are also released during volcanic eruptions. Though produced by natural phenomena, these gases have negative impacts on air and water quality similar to those that result from fossil fuel combustion.

The federal Acid Rain Program (ARP) has reduced SO_2 emissions by about 40 percent since 1990. Lakes and forests continue to show the effects of acidification, however, especially in the eastern United States. More than a quarter of all lakes in New York's Catskill Mountains are chronically acidic, prompting that state to introduce emergency measures to reduce acid rain. Beginning in the fall and winter of 2004–2005, electric utilities were required to reduce their emissions

to half the levels fixed in the ARP. Their compliance deadline was 2008. As of 2006, NO_x emissions had been reduced by almost 32 percent; SO_2 data for 2005–2007 showed a decline of more than 50 percent. Clearly, we are capable of improving environmental conditions if we choose! The ongoing challenge is that these emissions are carried over long distances. The Northeastern states are strongly affected by emissions that originate from states in the Midwest.

Carbon dioxide is another product of fossil fuel combustion. Data show that the concentration of CO_2 in the atmosphere has risen from 280 ppm, prior to the Industrial Revolution, to 380 ppm in 2008. This level does not reflect the fact that oceans absorb 30 percent of global CO_2. In ocean water, CO_2 forms carbonic acid and causes the release of hydrogen ions from water, which makes seawater more acidic. Carbonic acid dissolves calcium carbonate, the main component of coral exoskeletons. Higher concentrations of CO_2 in Earth's atmosphere also contribute to an increase in the greenhouse effect, which has been associated with changes in the world's climate. Increased water temperature results in an effect called coral bleaching, in which the corals' symbiotic algae die off, taking their colors with them. In 2005 researchers from the Center for Coastal Monitoring and Assessment observed coral reefs off the U.S. Virgin Islands, where water temperatures had been unusually warm. They found that 53 percent of coral reefs showed signs of bleaching. Some of these recovered in the following months; others were lost.

Running Dry

Water stress is a reduction in the amount or quality of available water. It can be the result of many factors, including climate, population increase, overuse, or pollution. California is one of many regions in the world that faces water stress because of a rapidly expanding population. Two-thirds of California's population live in the southern half of the state, mostly in the large metropolitan areas around Los Angeles and San Diego. Much of their water supply comes from mountain snowmelt in the northern and eastern parts of the state, and from the

Water coursing through this aqueduct is to serve Los Angeles, California.

Colorado River (part of which runs along the California-Arizona border). This water is transported for hundreds of miles in aqueducts (underground or aboveground canals). Likewise, much of the water supply for the 8.2 million residents of New York City comes from up to 125 miles (201 km) away. That city has nearby surface and groundwater supplies, but its massive population make them insufficient.

Americans are among the world's top consumers of water, using an average of 100 gallons (379 L) per person each day. This figure represents per capita (per person) water use in cities for drinking, cooking, bathing, landscaping, recreation, industry, and all other uses. People can get by with less, of course. Residents of Germany and France use less than 60 gallons (227 L) a day. Part of this disparity comes as a result of conservation. For example, many European nations routinely require low-flush toilets using 1.6-gallon (6-L) or smaller tanks. In the United States low-flush systems are increasing in popularity, and all new toilets are made to meet the low-flush standard. Many homes, however, still have older toilets (made before 1994) that use 3.5 to 8 gallons (13 to 30 L) for every flush. In a family of four, this can result in more than 14,000 gallons (53,000 L) of water wasted each year.

Domestic use of water is only a small part of any nation's total water consumption. Much, much more water is needed to provide the food we eat, manufacture things that make our lives comfortable, and produce electrical power. The U.S. Geological Survey (USGS) defines eight major categories of water use: public supply (city use), domestic (household use), irrigation, livestock, aquaculture (raising fish or shellfish), industrial, mining, and thermoelectric power. (Water in electrical power plants is used either to make steam that runs generating turbines, or as part of a cooling system.) In 2000 water use for the United States averaged 408 billion gallons per day (1.54 trillion L). Domestic use made up one percent of the total. Together, irrigation and thermoelectric power accounted for 82 percent.

Five

Managing for the Future

Results from the 2002 National Water Quality Inventory indicate that water quality problems continue to be associated with sediment, pathogens, nutrients, and organic enrichment. Once again, efforts must be stepped up to prevent nonpoint source pollution as well as sewage overflows and effluents. Another key objective is water conservation. Water managers also consider antidegradation an ongoing priority.

Saving Water
United States Supreme Court Justice Sandra Day O'Connor wrote, "There is recognition in the Clean Water Act itself that reduced stream flow, i.e., diminishment of water quantity, can constitute water pollution." Her comment related to a case in 1994 in which a utility company wanted to build a new hydro-power dam on the Dosewallips River in Washington State. The case went all the way to the Supreme Court because state ecologists insisted that the dam would remove too much water from the river, and therefore would harm fish populations. This case led to a landmark decision in environmental law. It confirmed the relationship between water quantity and water

quality, and clearly stated the government's responsibility to protect both. The utility company lost.

This clarification may have come just in time. Today, many communities are juggling demands for more water with real concerns about water scarcity. Governments and citizens in the Colorado River Basin are facing this exact problem. The Colorado River begins in northern Colorado's Rocky Mountain National Park, flowing through or along the borders of seven states before crossing into Mexico. Along its way, the great river supplies water to more than 25 million people in those states. River water is also used for irrigation, industry, and the production of electricity in two massive hydropower dams. Most of the Colorado's flow comes from snowmelt in the Rockies. A long drought that began in 1999 has caused runoff from the mountains to decline. The river and its major reservoirs—Lake Mead and Lake Powell—have fallen dramatically. As of 2008 both reservoirs contained less than half of the water they were designed to hold. As the drought continues, the potential for conflict between the states increases—especially because states downstream may receive less water if upstream states do not conserve.

Recognizing the need for action, in December 2007 the U.S. Department of the Interior promoted a twenty-year agreement between the seven Colorado River states. They have consented to work out any conflicts rather than go to court, and—perhaps more important—to implement water management strategies that will use available water in a fair and responsible way. Conservation is foremost among these strategies.

Las Vegas is one of the cities served by the Colorado River. A report prepared by the Pacific Institute in 2007 indicates that Las Vegas residents consume an average of 163 gallons (617 L) of water per day. This is down from 322 gallons (1,219 L) per day in 1997, but remains a third higher than water use in other desert cities such as Albuquerque or Tucson. The report also summarizes approaches that can be used to reduce consumption, including tax incentives for using conservation methods in new buildings, exchange programs that allow people to trade inefficient fixtures (such as toilet flappers and showerheads)

Glen Canyon Dam in Arizona forms Lake Powell. Low water levels in current years adversely affect those that depend on its waters.

for varieties that save water, and raising the price of water to reflect its actual value. (In economics, the law of supply and demand suggests that people will buy less if something costs more.) Public education is critically important if conservation efforts are to succeed—people need to know where water comes from, why it is valuable and limited, and how to conserve it.

Cities also have an obligation to reduce water use. Urban water is used to maintain governmental buildings, public landscaping, and much more. In 2008 the Solano County Water Agency, located north of San Francisco, set an example of how to reduce water usage within its boundaries. The county installed a "smart water management system," innovative new technology that can adjust the amount of water delivered to sprinklers on a day-to-day basis, depending on weather and other conditions. The agency expects to conserve 30 million gallons (113.5 million L) of water each year. Runoff pollution may be reduced by 71 percent, because grassy areas will not be irrigated beyond their ability to absorb the water applied.

Agricultural Best Practices

The U.S. EPA and agricultural experts also recommend a variety of best management practices (BMPs) to conserve water and protect water quality.

- Irrigation on farms accounts for most of the water used in the United States, and more than half of this goes to large farms. A common method of irrigation is to flood the fields and let water pour along furrows between rows of crops. This promotes erosion and runoff, which moves sediments and nutrients into local waterways. It also allows water to evaporate. Elevated sprinkler systems and drip systems reduce erosion and runoff. Agricultural experts recommend that such water-saving systems be installed on large farms.

- Farmers can leave bits of plants on fields after removing crops. This reduces erosion between plantings. It's ten times more effective to leave "standing residue"—pieces

This farm in Bakersfield, California, utilizes sprinkler-system irrigation, which reduces runoff and erosion.

of stems that are still rooted in the ground—than to plow everything under.

- Buffer strips also reduce erosion. These are rows of grasses, shrubs, or trees that border fields or streams.

Like wetlands, these can hold on to sediments and pollutants that would otherwise enter bodies of water. The U.S. Department of Agriculture reports that properly placed buffers can absorb up to 50 percent of nutrients and pesticides, 60 percent of pathogens, and 75 percent of sediments. They can also provide habitat for wild-life and much-needed privacy for farmers in otherwise open areas.

- Many fields receive much more nitrogen and phos-phorus, in the form of fertilizers and manure, than soils can hold. Nutrient management, also called pre-cision agriculture, is a technique that allows farmers to measure how many nutrients are needed in par-ticular parts of their fields. This prevents waste, expense, and pollution. Similarly, livestock are often given feed that contains more protein (which breaks down into nitrogen) and phosphorus than they can use. The remainder is lost in manure and urine. Pre-cision feeding can reduce the levels of nutrients lost in excreta, while maintaining the health of animals.

- Many pesticides are hazardous to both human health and to the environment. Integrated pest management (IPM) is an approach that can significantly reduce pesticide use. Pests must be identified before they are treated, so that inappropriate chemicals are not applied. Prevention techniques include practicing crop rotation, encouraging natural predators, and using pest-resistant plant varieties. Chemicals only are used when absolutely necessary, and then are targeted at the exact pest in the precise location of infestation.

- The U.S. EPA has required that animal feeding opera-tions (AFOs) with large numbers of animals, or whose facilities are close to water, obtain NPDES permits. Regardless of size, all AFOs must also develop nutrient management plans describing how they will control the discharge of nutrients, sediments, and pathogens into water. These plans cover precision feeding, handling and storing of manure, applying manure to land, conserving land and soil, dealing with runoff, handling dead animals, and keeping records of the operation.

Best management practices (BMPs) are not for agriculture alone—citizens should put them to use, as well. IPM can be used on lawns and gardens. Many chemical pesticides can be tracked into the house on clothes. They can be inhaled or absorbed through the skin. You may not use them, but your neighbor's pesticides can move through air and water to affect your property and health. BMPs for a healthy yard start with choosing a variety of grass that is right for the region—or better yet, no grass at all. There are approximately 40 million acres (16 million ha) of lawn in the United States, and Americans spend billions of dollars each year to keep them lush. Much of the upkeep given to lawns and gardens is water-intensive and unhealthy, involving chemicals that can harm wildlife and people. Solutions to this are simple. Fertilizers should never be applied if it looks like rain, as they will be lost in runoff. Instead, use compost and mulch to provide nutrients. Keep grass mowed at a high level to discourage weeds and increase infiltration. Just like farmers, gardeners need to be informed about pests in the yard before applying chemicals, which can kill beneficial insects if used incorrectly. Alternatively, use sprays made of garlic, onion, hot pepper, or even old-fashioned soap and water.

Slowing the Flow of Stormwater

The focus of water quality management has changed somewhat over the years. While toxic pollutants from industry once were the focus—and should still be monitored—the U.S. EPA now stresses that updated water quality standards should include numeric and narrative criteria for sediment levels, nutrients, and biological indicators. Local agencies and governments often focus on stormwater management to meet these standards. For example, cities may sweep streets to keep organic materials, pet excreta, and sediments out of storm sewers. Settlement ponds

are set up anywhere that runoff might be an issue: around highways, in urban and suburban areas, and near agricultural operations. These are shallow, man-made ponds that capture runoff water. As the water sits in a settlement pond, sediments and nutrients sink to the bottom. Cleaner water from the top can then be discharged into a local stream or lake.

Cities can also require developers to use stormwater-control practices on construction sites and in the buildings they create. Where sites have a lot of impervious surface, builders may be required to install underground basins to capture runoff. As an alternative, they might use permeable pavers, which are a relatively new building material that can be applied in parking lots and driveways to reduce impervious surface. When these small blocks are fitted together, spaces are left through which water can drain. Permeable asphalts are now available as well. Protecting the vegetation on hillsides, and alongside lakes and streams, is another important consideration of any construction project. Silt fencing keeps exposed construction sites from eroding, especially on hills that lead down to water. Good landscaping choices make a difference for water quality: trees catch falling rain and hold soil in place, reducing sedimentation and runoff, while grass allows a lot of runoff and usually requires fertilizer.

Some of the most exciting recent developments in stormwater management also have the benefit of looking fantastic. Buffers, rain gardens, and green roofs use vegetation to capture runoff and are making a significant difference in many cities and suburbs. Buffers are strips of unmowed native vegetation that can absorb sediments and nutrients. Like those used on farms, they control runoff and erosion, and provide important wildlife habitat. Landowners with waterside property may be interested in this: a study conducted on thirty-seven lakes in Minnesota showed that a 3-foot (1-m) change in water clarity significantly altered property values. Homeowners and cities are also using rain gardens to deal with runoff. These gardens are often small, consisting of only a shallow basin filled with compost and mulch, then planted with native grasses and wildflowers. If placed appropriately, such gardens can collect runoff from roofs, driveways, or parking lots. Water sits in the rain garden for a day or two while slowly infiltrating (but not standing long enough to encourage the growth of insect larvae such as mosquitoes). In 2003 rainwater gardens were installed in front of seventeen houses on a street in the suburb of Burnsville, Minnesota. Cuts were made into the curb in front of each, allowing runoff from the street (as well as from the houses) to flow in. Local storm sewers were fitted with monitors to measure the runoff. The street with rain gardens showed 90 percent less runoff than nearby streets without rain gardens.

The roof of Chicago's City Hall is a "green roof" in which gardens and plant life absorb runoff, sediment, and nutrients.

Green roofs use a similar approach—except that they are, literally, planted on rooftops. Using thin layers of light-weight soil and native plants that can survive high tempera-tures, designers are getting great results with these gardens. Home-owners can do this, but cities are jumping on board as well. Portland, Oregon, gets an average of 37 inches (94 cm) of rain a year. Portland requires publicly owned buildings to have green roofs wherever possible and has seen a 50 percent reduction in runoff from those structures. Chicago's city hall is capped with a garden, part of 3 million square feet (278,700 square m) of green roof space that is planned or already built in that city. And a 2.5-acre (1-ha) rolling green roof with seven hills crowns the top of the new California Academy of Sci-ences building in San Francisco's Golden Gate Park. Using native soils and plants, the designers of that garden hope to attract rare butterflies and other wildlife, as other green roofs have done. Along the way, green roofs can reduce by half the normally hellacious temperatures caused by gravel and black rooftops—which in turn lowers temperatures inside the build-ings. Energy savings always equal water quality protection. The cities of New York, Philadephia, and Los Angeles are also accepting the challenge by requiring large-scale "green" proj-ects. These offer a smart combination of stormwater runoff reductions and reuse of green space that promises to make city life a lot sweeter in the years to come.

A Blue Planet Forever?

The great American naturalist and explorer John Muir wrote, "When we try to pick out anything by itself, we find it hitched to everything else in the universe." He recognized that we are inti-mately connected to water, air, soil, and wildlife. We are also very fortunate. Today we have the knowledge to make good choices and the technology to back them up. Our grandchildren may depart Earth to explore other parts of space—but if we act responsibly now, they will have a beautiful blue planet to call home.

Chapter One

p. 7, "...dozens of photographs of Earth.": "Apollo 8 Mission Photography." Lunar and Planetary Institute, Universities Space Research Association, 2008. http://www.lpi. usra.edu/expmoon/Apollo8/AO8_Photography.html. (Accessed 9 January 2008)

p. 8, "... Mars once had liquid water.": Kraal, Erin R. et al. "Martian Stepped-Delta Formation by Rapid Water Release." *Nature*, 21 February 2008, pp. 973–976.

p. 8, "The total volume of water...": "Where Is Earth's Water Located?" U.S. Geological Survey, 1 February 2007. http://ga.water.usgs.gov/edu/earthwherewater.html. (Accessed 23 October 2007)

p. 8, "...a depth of more than 1.7 miles.": Suzuki, David, with Amanda McConnell. *The Sacred Balance: Rediscovering Our Place in Nature.* Amherst, NY: Prometheus Books, 1997, p. 52.

p. 8, "...liquid water currently covers...": Suzuki, *The Sacred Balance*, p. 52.

p. 8, "...a huge supply of water in the mantle...": Fitzpatrick, Tony. "3-D Seismic Model of Vast Water Reservoir

Revealed: Earth Mantle 'Ocean.'" Washington University in St. Louis, 7 February 2007. http://news-info.wustl.edu/news/page/normal/8222.html. (Accessed 14 February 2008)

p. 9,   "...96.5 percent—is in the oceans...": "Where Is Earth's Water Located?"

p. 10, "On average, 60 percent of human body weight...": Suzuki, *The Sacred Balance*, p. 59.

p. 10, "...each person needs about a gallon...": Sterling, Eleanor J. "Blue Planet Blues." *Natural History*, November 2007, p. 30.

p. 10, "...85 percent of the weight of an apple...": Strauss, Rochelle. *One Well: The Story of Water on Earth.* Tonawanda, NY: Kids Can Press, 2007, p. 10.

p. 10, "...the stem of a saguaro cactus...": Dimmitt, Mark A. "Cactaceae (cactus family)." Arizona-Sonora Desert Museum, 2007. http://www.desertmuseum.org/books/nhsd_cactus_.php. (Accessed 29 December 2007)

p. 10, "Average salinity in the oceans...": "Saline Water." U.S. Geological Survey, 30 August 2005. http://ga.water.usgs.gov/edu/saline.html. (Accessed 17 December 2007)

p. 10, "Salinity of the Great Salt Lake...": Leopold, Luna B. *Waters, Rivers and Creeks.* Sausalito, CA: University Science Books, 1997, p. 125.

p. 11, "...approximately four billion tons of salts...": Swenson, Herbert. "Why Is the Ocean Salty?" U.S. Geological Survey, n/d. http://www.palomar.edu/oceanography/salty_ ocean.htm. (Accessed 15 March 2008)

p. 11, "Less than 3 percent of all water...": "Where Is Earth's Water Located?"

p. 12, "...(EPA) has set two parts per billion...": "Consumer Factsheet on: Mercury." U.S. Environmental Protection Agency, 28 November 2006. http://epa.gov/OGWDW/ contaminants/dw_contamfs/mercury.html. (Accessed 23 November 2007)

p. 13, "This accounts for 99 percent... only 0.008 percent of the planet's total water supply...": "Where Is Earth's Water Located?"

p. 13, "...an average of 105,500 cubic miles...": Thomczak, Matthias. "Introduction to Oceanography: Lecture Notes—The Global Oceanic Heat Budget." Flinders University: School of Chemistry, Physics & Earth Science, 2000. http://www.es.flinders.edu.au/~ mattom/IntroOc/ lecture04.html. (Accessed 29 January 2008)

p. 14, "...a single birch tree may collect...": Strauss, *One Well*, p. 10.

p. 14, "Soil layers usually extend...": "What is Soil?" United States Department of Agriculture: Natural Resources Conservation Service, n/d. http://www.mo14.nc.nrcs.usda. gov/features/whatissoil.html. (Accessed 6 March 2008)

p. 15, "It might take thousands of years...": Pielou, E. C. *Fresh Water*. Chicago: The University of Chicago Press, 1998, p. 13.

p. 16, "In 2000, aquifers provided 21 percent...": "Ground Water Use in the United States." U.S. Geological Survey, 27 March 2006. http://ga.water.usgs.gov/edu/wugw. html. (Accessed 12 December 2007)

p. 16, "The Ogallala has an area of...": "Ogallala Aquifer." *Water Encyclopedia*, 2007. http://www.waterencyclopedia.com/ Oc-Po/Ogallala-Aquifer.html. (Accessed 6 March 2008)

p. 16, "Heavy use of water from the Ogallala...": Sterling, "Blue Planet Blues," p. 30.

p. 16, "In 1900, 1.6 billion people…": "Population Dynamics." Environmental Literacy Council, 7 January 2008. http://www.enviroliteracy.org/subcategory.php/30.html. (Accessed 19 March 2008)

p. 16, "In 1970 that number had more than…": "About the Remember 1970 Contest." U.S. Environmental Protection Agency, 14 January 2008. http://www.epa.gov/aging/remember1970/about.htm. (Accessed 19 March 2008)

p. 16, "…69 percent of the U.S. population… Forty percent of those North American cities…": Hobbs, Franks, and Nicole Stoops. *Demographic Trends in the 20th Century*. U.S. Census Bureau, November 2002. http://www.census.gov/prod/2002pubs/censr-4.pdf. (Accessed 10 January 2008)

p. 18, "…the Federal Water Pollution Control Act…": "EPA History: Water—The Challenge of the Environment." U.S. Environmental Protection Agency, 21 September 2007. http://www.epa.gov/history/topics/fwpca/05.htm. (Accessed 31 October 2007)

p. 19, "Polls conducted in 1971 showed…": Whitaker, Joan C. "Earth Day Recollections: What It Was Like When the Movement Took Off." *EPA Journal*, July/August 1988. U.S. Environmental Protection Agency. http://www.epa.gov/history/topics/earthday/10.htm. (Accessed 2 November 2007)

p. 19, "Senator Edmund Muskie of Maine…": Robert W. Adler et al. *The Clean Water Act 20 Years Later*. Washington, DC: Island Press, 1993, p. 2.

p. 19, "It is the policy of the Congress…": *Federal Water Pollution Control Act*, U.S. Environmental Protection Agency, 8 March 2008, p. 3. http://www.epa.gov/region5/water/pdf/ecwa.pdf. (Accessed 10 March 2008)

Chapter Two

p. 21, "Dutch colonists in the 1600s...": McCully, Besty. *City at the Water's Edge: A Natural History of New York.* New Brunswick, NJ: Rivergate Books, 2007, pp. 80–83.

p. 21, "At the time of colonial settlement... By the 1980s, less than half of the wetlands...": Dahl, Thomas E., and Gregory J. Allord. "History of Wetlands in the Conterminous United States." U.S. Geological Survey, 7 March 1997. http://water. usgs.gov/nwsum/WSP2425/ history.html. (Accessed 30 November 2007)

p. 21, "Ninety-one percent of that state's wetlands...": Caduto, Michael J. *Pond and Brook: A Guide to Nature in Freshwater Environments.* Hanover, NH: University Press of New England, 1990, p. 212.

p. 22, "About 138 species of birds...": Stewart, Robert E. Jr. "Technical Aspects of Wetlands: Wetlands as Bird Habitat." U.S. Geological Survey, 7 September 2007. http://water.usgs.gov/nwsum/WSP2425/birdhabitat. html. (Accessed 28 February 2008)

p. 23, "The filtration system of wetlands is so effective...": Weller, Milton W. *Freshwater Marshes: Ecology and Wildlife Management, Second Edition.* Minneapolis, MN: University of Minnesota Press, 1987, pp. 101–102.

p. 25, "Crater Lake combines both factors.": "Crater Lake, Oregon." Volcano World and the North Dakota and Oregon Space Grant Consortia, n/d. http://volcano.und. edu/vwdocs/volc_images/north_america/crater_lake. html. (Accessed 1 March 2008)

p. 28, "Zebra mussels grow in large colonies...": "Nonindigenous Aquatic Species: Zebra Mussel." U.S. Geological Survey, 30 August 2007. http://nas.er.usgs. gov/queries/FactSheet.asp? speciesID = 95. (Accessed 23 February 2008)

p. 27, "A study done in British Columbia…": Shrimpton, J. M. et al. "Removal of the Riparian Zone During Forest Harvesting Increases Stream Temperature: Are the Effects Cumulative Downstream?" *Proceedings of a Conference on the Biology and Management of Species and Habitat at Risk, 15–19 February 1999.* British Columbia, Canada: B.C. Ministry of Environment, Lands, and Parks and University College of the Cariboo, 2000. http://wlapwww.gov.bc.ca/wld/documents/re09shrimpton.pdf. (Accessed 29 January 2008)

p. 28, "Today, the annual cost…": "Invasive Species in the Chesapeake Bay Watershed: A Workshop to Develop Regional Invasive Species Management Strategies." Chesapeake Bay Program and Maryland Sea Grant, 2002. http://www.mdsg.umd.edu/issues/restoration/non-natives/workshop/. (Accessed 23 February 2008)

p. 29, "A second invasive mussel…": "Nonindigenous Aquatic Species: Quagga Mussel." U.S. Geological Survey, 30 August 2007. http://nas.er.usgs.gov/queries/FactSheet.asp? speciesID = 95. (Accessed 23 February 2008)

p. 29, "In 2007, as many as 8,500 birds…": Janega, James. "Botulism Takes Fatal Toll on Thousands of Great Lakes Birds." *Chicago Tribune*, 15 January 2008. http://www.chicago tribune.com/news/chi-loons_ 15jan15,0,1170225.story. (Accessed 23 January 2008)

p. 31, "… (19,924 kilometers) of coastline…": "The World Factbook: United States." Central Intelligence Agency, 20 March 2008. https://www.cia.gov/library/publications/the-world-factbook/geos/us.html. (Accessed 20 March 2008)

p. 31, "Eelgrass beds are home…": Stout, Prentice K. "Eelgrass (*Zostera marina*): Flowering Plants of the Sea." Rhode Island Sea Grant, n/d. http://seagrant.gso.uri.edu/factsheets/eelgrass.html. (Accessed 10 February 2008)

p. 31, "Kelp beds grow like forests…": "Habitats: Kelp Forest." Olympic Coast National Marine Sanctuary, n/d. http:// olympiccoast.noaa.gov/living/habitats/kelpforest/ welcome.html. (Accessed 10 February 2008)

p. 31, "Coral reefs are built…": "Coastal Watershed Factsheets: Coral Reefs and Your Coastal Watershed." U.S. Environmental Protection Agency, 30 August 2007. http://www.epa.gov/owow/oceans/factsheets/fact4. html. (Accessed 10 February 2008)

p. 33, "When exploring a stream…": Bouchard, R. W. Jr. *Guide to Aquatic Invertebrates of the Upper Midwest: Identification Manual for Students, Citizen Monitors, and Aquatic Resource Professionals.* Saint Paul, MN: University of Minnesota, 2004.

Chapter Three

p. 36, "…to restore and maintain…": *Federal Water Pollution Control Act*, p. 3.

p. 38, "According to the EPA, nonpoint…": "What Is Nonpoint Source (NPS) Pollution? Questions and Answers." U.S. Environmental Protection Agency, 7 March 2008. http://www.epa.gov/owow/nps/qa.html. (Accessed 15 March 2008)

p. 39, "These consist of three components…": "What Are Water Quality Standards?" U.S. Environmental Protection Agency, 4 March 2008. http://www.epa.gov/waterscience/ standards/about/. (Accessed 6 March 2008)

p. 39, "…public water supplies, propagation…": *Federal Water Pollution Control Act*, p. 102.

p. 39, "The designated uses for Utah's…": Great Salt Lake Water Quality Steering Committee. "Purposes and Objectives." Utah Department of Environmental Quality, 18 August 2004. http://www.deq.utah.gov/ Issues/GSL_WQSC/. (Accessed 9 February 2008)

p. 39, "The Columbia River in Washington...": "Designated Beneficial Uses: Mainstem Columbia River." Oregon Department of Environmental Quality, November 2003. http://www.deq.state.or.us/wq/rules/div041/ dbutables/ table101a.pdf. (Accessed 10 February 2008)

p. 42, "Compliance monitoring...Ambient monitoring...": U.S. Environmental Protection Agency. *Overview of Watershed Monitoring*, Watershed Academy Web, 24 January 2007. http://www.epa.gov/watertrain/monitoring/. (Accessed 23 April 2007)

p. 42, "...the discharge of any pollutant...": *Federal Water Pollution Control Act*, p. 86.

p. 44, "Each permit applicant must show...": Killam, Gayle. *The Clean Water Act Owner's Manual, Second Edition.* Washington, DC: River Network, 2005, pp. 55–57.

p. 45, "...EPA's 2006 Toxics Release Inventory...": "2006 Toxics Release Inventory (TRI) Public Data Release Brochure." U.S. Environmental Protection Agency, 21 February 2008. http://www.epa.gov/tri/tridata/ tri06/brochure/brochure.htm. (Accessed 29 February 2008)

p. 47, "States must also prepare a Section 303(d) list...": *The Clean Water Act Owner's Manual*, Killam, pp. 92–108.

p. 47, "A State shall, to the maximum...": *Federal Water Pollution Control Act*, p. 172.

p. 48, "...pipe, ditch, channel, tunnel...": *Federal Water Pollution Control Act*, p. 211.

p. 48, "Control of stormwater runoff...": "Phases of the NPDES Stormwater Program." U.S. Environmental Protection Agency, 10 January 2008. http://cfpub.epa.gov/npdes/ stormwater/swphases.cfm. (Accessed 6 February 2008)

p. 49, "…Americans obtain their drinking water…": Woodson, R. Dodge. *Water Wells and Septic Systems Handbook.* New York: McGraw-Hill Professional, 2003, p. xix.

p. 49, "In 2007, there were 156,000 public drinking…roughly 68 percent of drinking water…": "Factoids: Drinking Water and Ground Water Statistics for 2007." U.S. Environmental Protection Agency, March 2008. http://www.epa.gov/safewater/data/pdfs/data_factoids_2007.pdf. (Accessed 8 May 2008)

p. 51, "As of 2008, the EPA had set MCLs…": "Drinking Water Contaminants." U.S. Environmental Protection Agency, 28 November 2006. http://www.epa.gov/safewater/ hfacts.html. (Accessed 21 September 2007)

p. 51, "…about 45 % of assessed stream miles…": "The National Water Quality Inventory: Report to Congress, 2002 Reporting Cycle." U.S. Environmental Protection Agency, October 2007. http://www.epa.gov/305b/2002report/. (Accessed 27 December 2007)

p. 54, "Many of these relate to water quality.": "Laws that We Administer." U.S. Environmental Protection Agency, 6 March 2008. http://www.epa.gov/lawsregs/laws/index.html. (Accessed 18 March 2008)

Chapter Four

p. 56, "In suburban areas, land cover averages…": "Limiting Impervious Surfaces Protects Water Quality." *Streamlines*, July 1996. http://h2o.enr.state.nc.us/wswp/SL/v1n5.html. (Accessed 8 March 2008)

p. 56, "The health of streams is impacted by…": Giannotti, Laurie, and Sandy Prisloe. "Do it Yourself! Impervious Surface Buildout Analysis." University of Connecticut Cooperative Extension System, 2002. http://nemo.uconn.edu/tools/publications/tech_papers/tech_paper_4.pdf. (Accessed 19 January 2008)

p. 56, "...about 16 percent of water can infiltrate... More than 80 percent of precipitation...": Marx, Josh et al. "The Relationship Between Soil and Water: How Soil Amendments and Compost Can Aid In Salmon Recovery." Soils for Salmon/Washington Organic Recycling Council, 1999. http://www.soilsforsalmon. org/why.htm. (Accessed 2 March 2008)

p. 57, "...the temperature on a gravel roof...": Marinelli, Janet. "Green Roofs Take Root." *National Wildlife*, December–January 2008, pp. 31–35.

p. 58, "...in 2001, 184 trout were found dead...": "Water Quality Improvement Plan for McLoud Run, Linn County, Iowa—Total Maximum Daily Load for Thermal Modifications." Iowa Department of Natural Resources, Water Improvement Section, 2007. http://www.iowadnr.com/water/watershed/tmdl/files/final/mcloudrun.pdf. (Accessed 23 December 2007)

p. 58, "A study at the University of Idaho...": "BMPs for Erosion Control." University of Idaho Extension, 3 January 2003. http://www.uidaho.edu/wq/wqbr/wqbr 27.html. (Accessed 19 January 2008)

p. 58, "Sediments also can be harmful to organisms...": Berry, Walter et al. "The Biological Effects of Suspended and Bedded Sediment (SABS) in Aquatic Systems: A Review." U.S. Environmental Protection Agency, 20 August 2003. http://www.epa.gov/waterscience/criteria/sediment/index.htm. (Accessed 9 January 2008)

p. 58, "...DDT...": Glenn, Bill. "U.S. EPA Acts to Speed Cleanup of DDT-Contaminated Sediment." U.S. Environmental Protection Agency, 16 December 1996. http://www.epa.gov/epahome/search.html. (Accessed 14 December 2007)

p. 58, "…mercury, arsenic…": *San Francisco Bay Water Quality Index*, The Bay Institute, 17 October 2003. http://www.bay.org/Scorecard/Water_Quality.pdf. (Accessed 14 December 2007)

p. 60, "…DDT, in the 1940s during World War II…": "DDT Ban Takes Effect—EPA Press Release, December 31, 1972." U.S. Environmental Protection Agency, 21 September 2007. http://www.epa.gov/history/topics/ddt/01.htm. (Accessed 13 February 2008)

p. 60, "In 2000 pesticide use in the United States….": "2000–2001 Pesticide Market Estimates: Usage." U.S. Environmental Protection Agency, 24 July 2007. http://www.epa.gov/oppbead1/pestsales/01pestsales/usage2001.htm. (Accessed 19 November 2007)

p. 62, "Glyphosate, a commonly used organophosphate herbicide…": "Glyphosate Herbicide Found in Many Midwestern Streams, Antibiotics Not Common." U.S. Geological Survey, 20 February 2008. http://toxics.usgs.gov/highlights/glyphosate02.html. (Accessed 9 March 2008)

p. 62, "…hormonal changes in male frogs…": Sanders, Robert. "Popular Weed Killer Atrazine Feminizes Native Frogs Across Midwest, Could Be Impacting Amphibian Populations Worldwide." *University of California-Berkeley, Campus News*, 30 October 2002. http://www.berkeley.edu/news/media/releases/2002/10/30_frogs.html. (Accessed 20 February 2008)

p. 62, "…Centers for Disease Control cautions…": "Public Health Statement: Atrazine." Agency for Toxic Substances and Disease Registry, n/d. http://www.atsdr.cdc.gov/toxprofiles/tp153-c1.pdf. (Accessed 20 February 2008)

p. 62, "…agricultural chemicals are monitored…": "Federal Insecticide, Fungicide and Rodenticide Act (FIFRA)

Enforcement." U.S. Environmental Protection Agency, 31 October 2007. http://www.epa.gov/compliance/ civil/fifra/index.html. (Accessed 5 December 2007)

p. 63, "...the average size of the Gulf hypoxic zone...": *Gulf Hypoxia Action Plan 2008, Draft for Public Review.* U.S. Environmental Protection Agency, 9 November 2007. http://www.epa.gov/msbasin/. (Accessed 3 January 2008)

p. 63, "...manure: 500 million tons... Four percent of AFOs": Gluckman, Matt. "EPA Regional CAFO Waste Issues." U.S. Environmental Protection Agency, 2007. http:// es.epa.gov/ncer/publications/workshop/pdf/gluckman_ region582007.pdf. (Accessed 17 March 2008)

p. 64, "The Chesapeake Bay is...": Horton, Tom. "Saving the Chesapeake." *National Geographic,* June 2005, pp. 22–45.

p. 65, "In 1983, a report ordered by Congress...": "1983 Chesapeake Bay Agreement." Chesapeake Bay Program, 27 July 1999. http:// www.chesapeakebay.net/content/ publications/ cbp_ 12512.pdf. (Accessed 28 November 2007)

p. 65, "Pennsylvania has made strides...": "Pennsylvania Makes Progress; Takes Leadership Role on Chesapeake Bay Restoration Efforts." PR Newswire, 5 December 2007. http://media.prnewswire.com/. (Accessed 11 December 2007)

p. 66, "In the mid–1800s these cities put in combined sewer...": Schladweiler, Jon C. "Tracking Down the Roots of Our Sanitary Sewers: The New American Roots." Arizona Water & Pollution Control Association, 2004. http:// www.sewerhistory.org/chronos/new_amer_roots.htm. (Accessed 23 January 2008)

p. 66, "...declines in the productivity of oyster beds...": McCully, *City at the Water's Edge,* p. 84.

p. 66, "Bacteria levels in the Hudson River…": Adler, *The Clean Water Act 20 Years Later*, p. 5.

p. 66, "Sewage piped into Lake Erie…": Steinberg, Ted. *Down to Earth: Nature's Role in American History.* New York: Oxford University Press, 2002, pp. 166–168.

p. 66, "In early 1906, 2,300 people in Philadelphia…": "Philadelphia Water Peril." *New York Times*, 26 February 1906. http://www.nytimes.com/. (Accessed 17 December 2007)

p. 66, "…Dr. John Snow had discovered in 1848 that typhoid…": Jesperson, Kathy. "Drinking Water History." *On Tap*, 1996–1997. http://www.nesc.wvu.edu/ndwc/ndwc_dwhistory.html. (Accessed 22 October 2007)

p. 67, "Philadelphia dealt with this problem in 1909…": "Urban Water Cycle: Water Treatment." City of Philadelphia, n/d. http://www.phila.gov/water/urban_water_cycle.html. (Accessed 22 October 2007)

p. 67, "Combined sewer systems serve approximately…": "2004 Combined Sewer Overflow Statistically-Valid Noncompliance Rate Study." U.S. Environmental Protection Agency, 25 January 2008. http://www.epa.gov/oecaerth/data/planning/priorities/ cwacsosvcrstudy.html. (Accessed 13 February 2008)

p. 67, "…there were almost 20,000 health advisories…": Angelos, William. "Polluted Water Cause of Costly Beach Closures." *Daily News Central*, 29 July 2005. http://health.dailynewscentral.com/content/view/1383/63. (Accessed 26 January 2008)

p. 68, "…Chicago's colossal Stickney…": "District Facilities." Metropolitan Water Reclamation District of Greater Chicago, 18 October 2001. http://www.mwrdgc.dst.il.us/plants/default.htm. (Accessed 19 March 2008)

p. 68, "...it is burned, sent to a landfill...95 percent free of contaminants...": Alters, Sandra. *Garbage and Other Pollution.* Farmington Hills, MI: Gale Group, Inc., 2002, p. 96.

p. 70, "If more than five samples per month...": "Total Coliform Rule: Basic Information." U.S. Environmental Protection Agency, 13 July 2007. http://epa.gov/SAFEWATER/disinfection/tcr/basicinformation.html. (Accessed 20 January 2008)

p. 70, "*Cryptosporidium* is much more difficult to remove...": Kneen, Barbara et al. "Cryptosporidium: A Waterborne Pathogen." *Water Treatment Notes*, USDA Water Quality Program, August 2004. http://hosts.cce.cornell.edu/wq-fact-sheets/Fspdf/Factsheet15_RS.pdf. (Accessed 12 February 2008)

p. 70, "As of 1988, almost ten percent...": Adler et al. *The Clean Water Act Twenty Years Later*, p. 14.

p. 70, "About one in four Americans...": "Septic (Onsite) Systems." U.S. Environmental Protection Agency, n/d. http://cfpub.epa.gov/owm/septic/index.cfm. (Accessed 13 February 2008)

p. 70, "The Blue Earth River watershed...": Steil, Mark. "Blue Earth River Heavily Polluted." Minnesota Public Radio, 9 June 2005. http://news.minnesota.publicradio.org/features/2005/06/09_steilm_blueearth/. (Accessed 14 March 2008)

p. 71, "...Catskill Mountains are chronically acidic...": "DEC Adopts Emergency Rules Regarding Acid Rain." New York State Department of Environmental Conservation, September 2004. http://www.dec.ny.gov/environmentdec/18654.html. (Accessed 13 December 2007)

p. 72, "As of 2006, NO$_x$ emissions…": "New York State Total SO$_2$ and NO$_x$ Emissions From Electric Generating Facilities." Personal communication, Rob Sliwinski, New York Bureau of Air Quality Planning, 23 January 2008.

p. 72, "…CO$_2$ in the atmosphere has risen…": Tedesco, Kathy et al. "Impacts of Anthropogenic CO$_2$ on Ocean Chemistry and Biology." NOAA's Office of Oceanic and Atmospheric Research, 3 October 2005. http://www.research.noaa.gov/spotlite/spot_gcc.html. (Accessed 15 December 2007)

p. 72, "…coral reefs off the U.S. Virgin Islands…": Jeffrey, Christopher et al. "Coral Bleaching and Recovery Observed at Buck Island, St. Croix, U.S. Virgin Islands, October and December, 2005." Center for Coastal Monitoring and Assessment, 3 April 2006. http://ccma.nos.noaa.gov/products/biogeography/coral_bleaching/welcome.html. (Accessed 15 January 2008)

p. 72, "Two-thirds of California's population…": "Introduction: The State Water Project." California Department of Water Resources, n/d. http://www.swpao.water.ca.gov/publications/bulletin/95/view/text/ intro.htm. (Accessed 16 February 2008)

p. 74, "…8.2 million residents of New York City…": "City of New York/Multi-County Partnership: Protecting Drinking Water." The United States Conference of Mayors, 1998. http://www.usmayors.org/uscm/best_practices/bp97/12_1997_Protecting_Drinking_Water.htm. (Accessed 19 February 2008)

p. 74, "…an average of 100 gallons per person…": Hinrichsen, Don. "Water Pressure." *National Wildlife*, June/July 2004. http://www.nwf.org/nationalwildlife/printerFriendly.cfm?issueID = 68& articleID = 928. (Accessed 4 December 2007)

p. 74, "Residents of Germany and France...": Hinrichsen, "Water Pressure."

p. 74, "...3.5 to 8 gallons for every flush.": Waskom, R., and M. Neibauer. "Water Conservation In and Around the Home." Colorado State University Extension, 4 March 2008. http://www.ext.colostate.edu/pubs/consumer/09952.html. (Accessed 11 March 2008)

p. 74, "...eight major categories of water use...": Hutson, Nancy L. et al. *Estimated Use of Water in the United States in 2000.* U.S. Geological Survey, February 2005. http://pubs.usgs.gov/circ/2004/circ1268/htdocs/text-intro.html. (Accessed 24 December 2007)

Chapter Five
p. 75, "...there is recognition in the Clean Water Act...": "U.S. Supreme Court: Jefferson City PUD v. Ecology Dept. of Washington, 1994." FindLaw.com, n/d. http://laws.findlaw.com/us/511/700.html. (Accessed 19 November 2007)

p. 76, "The Colorado provides water for...": "Colorado River Programs and Projects." U.S. Department of the Interior, 10 January 2008. http://www.doi.gov/issues/colorado.html. (Accessed 27 February 2008)

p. 76, "A long drought that began in 1999...": Clayton, Rick. "Lake Powell-Glen Canyon Dam: Current Status." U.S. Bureau of Reclamation, 5 February 2008. http://www.usbr.gov/uc/water/crsp/cs/gcd.html. (Accessed 27 February 2008)

p. 76, "...in December 2007 the U.S. Department...": "Colorado River Programs and Projects."

p. 76, "A report prepared by the Pacific Institute...": Cooley, Heather et al. "Hidden Oasis: Water Conservation and Efficiency in Las Vegas." The Pacific Institute,

November 2007. http://www.pacinst.org/reports/las_ vegas/. (Accessed 1 March 2008)

p. 78, "...the Solano County Water Agency...": "Solano County Water Agency Quells Thirsty Landscapes With WeatherTRAK® Smart Water Management." WeatherTRAK.com, 12 December 2007. http:// www.weathertrak.com/weathertrak-updates/press- 20071212.php. (Accessed 12 December 2007)

p. 78, "The EPA and agricultural experts also recommend...": "Agricultural Management Practices for Water Quality Protection: Introduction." U.S. Environmental Protection Agency, 4 January 2007. http://www.epa.gov/watertrain/ agmodule/. (Accessed 18 November 2007)

p. 78, "Irrigation on farms accounts for...": Schaible, Glenn. "Irrigation, Water Conservation, and Farm Size in the Western United States." *Amber Waves,* June 2004. http:// www.ers.usda.gov/AmberWaves/June04/findings/ IrrigationWestern.htm. (Accessed 14 February 2008)

p. 78, "It's ten times more effective...": McGraw, Linda, and Dan Comb. "Standing Crop Residue for Erosion Control." *Agricultural Research,* July 2000. http://findarticles.com/p/ articles/mi_m3741/is_7_48/ai_63986955. (Accessed 1 March 2008)

p. 80, "The U.S. Department of Agriculture reports...": "Buffer Strips: Common Sense Conservation." USDA Natural Resources Conservation Service, n/d. http:// www.nrcs.usda. gov/FEATURE/buffers/. (Accessed 1 March 2008)

p. 80, "...precision agriculture, is a technique that...": McGinnis, Laura. "Precision Agriculture Systems: Maximizing Benefits with Better Management." *Agricultural Research,* March 2007. http://www.ars.usda.gov/is/AR/archive/ mar07/agric0307.htm. (Accessed 27 October 2007)

p. 80, "...feed that contains more protein...and phosphorus...":
Rotz, C. A. et al. "Feeding Strategy, Nitrogen Cycling, and
Profitability of Dairy Farms." *Journal of Dairy Science*, v.
82 n. 12, 1999, pp. 2841–2855. http://jds.fass.org/cgi/
content/abstract/82/12/2841. (Accessed 18 December
2007)

p. 80, "...feed that contains more protein...and phosphorus...":
Cerosaletti, P. E. et al. "Phosphorus Reduction Through
Precision Feeding of Dairy Cattle." *Journal of Dairy
Science*, v. 87, 2004, pp. 2314–2323. http://jds.fass.org/
cgi/content/abstract/87/7/2314. (Accessed 18 December
2007)

p. 80, "Integrated   Pest   Management   (IPM)   is...":
"Integrated Pest Management (IPM) Principles." U.S.
Environmental Protection Agency, 13 March 2008.
http://www.epa.gov/opp00001/factsheets/ipm.htm.
(Accessed 17 March 2008)

p. 80, "The   EPA   has   required   that   animal   feeding
operations...": Telega, Stanley, and Peg Cook. "Fact
Sheet #5: What If My Operation is an AFO But Not a
CAFO?" General Information. Livestock and Poultry
Environmental Stewardship Curriculum, 2003. http://
www.lpes.org/CAFO.html. (Accessed 29 January 2008)

p. 81, "...approximately 40 million acres of lawn...": Thacker,
Paul D. "American Lawns Impact Nutrient Cycles."
Science News, 16 February 2005. http://pubs.acs.org/
subscribe/journals/esthag-w/2005/feb/science/pt_
lawns.html. (Accessed 18 October 2007)

p. 81, "...updated water quality standards should include...":
"What Are Water Quality Standards?: Water Quality
Criteria." U.S. Environmental Protection Agency,
5 December 2006. http://www.epa.gov/waterscience/
standards/about/crit.htm. (Accessed 20 March 2008)

p. 82, "A study conducted on thirty-seven lakes…": Krysel, Charles et al. *Lakeshore Property Values and Water Quality: Evidence From Property Sales in the Mississippi Headwaters Region.* Mississippi Headwaters Board and Bemidji State University, 14 May 2003. http://www. co.cass.mn.us/esd/intralake/bsu_study.pdf (Accessed 17 March 2008)

p. 83, "In 2003 rainwater gardens were installed…": "Burnsville Rainwater Gardens." *Land and Water*, v. 51 n. 5, September/October 2007. http://www.landand water. com/features/vol48no5/vol48no5_2.php. (Accessed 13 December 2007)

p. 83, "Portland, Oregon, gets an average…": Tweit, Susan J. "Raising the Roof." *Audubon*, March–April 2008, pp. 40–46.

p. 83, "Chicago's city hall is capped with a garden…": Marinelli, Janet. "Green Roofs Take Root." *National Wildlife*, December/January 2008, pp. 31–35.

p. 83, "When we try to pick out anything by itself…": Muir, John. *My First Summer in the Sierra.* San Francisco: Sierra Club Books, 1988, p. 100.

Further Information

Books

Bowden, Rob. *Earth's Water Crisis*. Milwaukee, WI: World Almanac Library, 2007.

Fridell, Ron. *Environmental Issues*. New York: Marshall Cavendish Benchmark, 2006.

Jacobson, Robert. *Water: No Longer Taken for Granted*. Wylie, TX: Information Plus, 2006.

O'Connor, Rebecca. *Acid Rain*. Farmington Hills, MI: Lucent Books, 2004.

Warhol, Tom. *Water*. New York: Marshall Cavendish Benchmark, 2006.

Websites

National Oceanic and Atmospheric Administration (NOAA)

www.noaa.gov/

NOAA is the best source for data and information about coastlines, oceans, fisheries, and weather.

U.S. EPA: High School Environmental Center

www.epa.gov/highschool/water.htm

The United States Environmental Protection Agency (EPA) provides a massive list of current links to water-related websites.

U.S. EPA: Water Quality Criteria for Nutrient and Phosphorus Pollution

www.epa.gov/waterscience/criteria/nutrient

Select the "Where You Live" link to navigate through an up-to-date database of information about water quality standards, impairments, and ecological information for each state and U.S. territory.

Water Resources of the United States

water.usgs.gov/

Visit the U.S. Geological Survey (USGS) to obtain data about groundwater, surface water, water use, and water quality.

World Water Monitoring Day

www.worldwatermonitoringday.us/

Does your school or club monitor water quality on a local stream, lake, or estuary? This site offers affordable water monitoring kits. Most important, your results can be posted to the online database and compared with data about water quality in more than forty countries.

Bibliography

Adler, Robert W. et al. *The Clean Water Act 20 Years Later*. Washington, DC: Island Press, 1993.

Alters, Sandra. *Garbage and Other Pollution*. Farmington Hills, MI: Gale Group, 2002.

Bouchard, R. W. Jr. *Guide to Aquatic Invertebrates of the Upper Midwest: Identification Manual for Students, Citizen Monitors, and Aquatic Resource Professionals*. Saint Paul, MN: University of Minnesota, 2004.

Caduto, Michael J. *Pond and Brook: A Guide to Nature in Freshwater Environments*. Hanover, NH: University Press of New England, 1990.

Carlsen, William S., Nancy M. Trautman, and the Environmental Inquiry Team. *Watershed Dynamics*. Arlington, VA: NSTA Press, 2004.

Jacobson, Robert, and Paula Kepos. *Water: No Longer Taken For Granted*. Wylie, TX: Information Plus, 2006.

Killam, Gayle. *The Clean Water Act Owner's Manual, Second Edition*. Washington, DC: River Network, 2005.

Leopold, Luna B. *Waters, Rivers and Creeks*. Sausalito, CA: University Science Books, 1997.

McCully, Betsy. *City at the Water's Edge: A Natural History of New York*. New Brunswick, NJ: Rivergate Books, 2007.

Pielou, E. C. *Fresh Water*. Chicago: The University of Chicago Press, 1998.

Starke, Linda (Ed.) *State of the World, 2006: A Worldwatch Institute Report on Progress Toward a Sustainable Society*. Washington, DC: Worldwatch Institute, 2006.

Steinberg, Ted. *Down to Earth: Nature's Role in American History*. New York: Oxford University Press, 2002.

Suzuki, David, with Amanda McConnell. *The Sacred Balance: Rediscovering Our Place in Nature*. Amherst, NY: Prometheus Books, 1997.

Weller, Milton W. *Freshwater Marshes: Ecology and Wildlife Management, Second Edition*. Minneapolis: University of Minnesota Press, 1987.

Woodson, R. Dodge. *Water Wells and Septic Systems Handbook*. New York: McGraw-Hill Professional, 2003.

Pages in **boldface** are illustrations

About the Author

Christine Petersen is a freelance writer and environmental educator who lives near Minneapolis, Minnesota. As a middle school science teacher, Petersen spent four years developing a water quality study for her school's service-learning program. She now volunteers as the chair of her local watershed district's citizen advisory committee, and monitors water quality in the lake she lives beside. When she's not writing, Petersen spends time with her young son and enjoys snowshoeing, kayaking, and birding. She is a member of the Society of Children's Book Writers and Illustrators, and is the author of more than two dozen books for young people.